THE ERA OF THE FRENCH REVOLUTION, 1789-1799
Ten Years That Shook the World

LE(

Pro

Nev

AN ANVIL ORIGINAL
under the general editorship of
LOUIS L. SNYDER

KRIEGER PUBLISHING COMPANY
MALABAR, FLORIDA

Original Edition 1957
Reprint Edition 1984

Distributed by:
Marvin Melnyk Assoc. Ltd.
Queenston, Ontario L0S 1L0
905 262-4964 Fax 262-4963

Printed in the United States of America

Library of Congress Cataloging in Publication Data

Gershoy, Leo,
    The era of the French Revolution, 1789-1799.

    Reprint. Originally published: New York: Van Nostrand, c1957.
    Bibliography: p.
    Includes index.
    1. France—History—Revolution, 1789-1799.
I. Title.
DC149.G43   1984   944.04   83-22235
ISBN 0-89874-718-X

10   9   8   7   6   5   4   3

PREFACE

As the title of this small book suggests, the French Revolution was much more than a revolution in France. It was, of course, within the country of its origin, an upheaval which shattered the structure of royal absolutism and forever destroyed a social order based upon aristocratic privilege. It became the central social and psychological fact in French history for the following hundred years.

Nevertheless, the French Revolution was also a central fact in the history of Europe and the western world, the most significant and the most comprehensive of the several revolutions that occurred in the later eighteenth century. Outside France, for reasons that varied according to the region, up to 1789 the protests of the nonprivileged social groups had been stilled and the aspirations of liberal reformers denied. When the Revolution broke out in France, its doctrines were already familiar and dear to the progressives of the neighboring states. These admirers hailed its achievements, organizing themselves, too, where they could for political action.

The ten years from 1789 to 1799 which are examined here saw only the beginning of revolutionary change in Europe. In most of the states the Revolution was less welcomed than almost hysterically rejected during this decade. But it had the whole nineteenth century in which to work. For the practices of princely absolutism the revolutionaries substituted the principles of political liberty and government by discussion. In the place of the class society dating back to mediaeval days which prevailed everywhere on the continent, they introduced a social order based on the equality of man. No one who has studied their work will attempt to deny that they advanced ideals which they failed to live up to, and that they made many mistakes and committed many crimes. But for a simple reason the ideals by which they were

3

moved made history: they were part of a larger world pattern of hopes and developments, of a movement from less liberty to more, from privilege to equality, from aristocracy to democracy.

Since the most important documents, such as laws and decrees, constitutions, treaties, and official governmental reports, are readily available in several collections, of which J. H. Stewart's *A Documentary Survey of the French Revolution* is the most useful, I have deliberately kept their number to a minimum in this book. It will be noted that the title of Part II is *Readings* and not *Documents*. Where possible or desirable, I have tried to include selections from nonofficial contemporary sources, such as newspapers, letters, diaries, treatises, many of which have not been translated before. While both readings and documents have been abridged, every effort has been made not to distort their meaning or change their emphasis. Obviously, each author follows his own inclinations in the selections that he makes no matter how much he afterwards rationalizes the choices that he presents to the reader. My own rationalization consists of the hope that the selections I have made will give the reader a sense of the immediacy of revolutionary change which more formal documents cannot possibly give.

Not for the first time in my experience as author I drew heavily upon my wife's fund of patient competence. My gratitude for her help in the writing of this book is great.

New York University   LEO GERSHOY

TABLE OF CONTENTS

Part I

THE ERA OF THE
FRENCH REVOLUTION, 1789–1799
Ten Years That Shook The World

— 1 —

INTRODUCTION

THE SCOPE AND SIGNIFICANCE
OF THE FRENCH REVOLUTION

The first accounts of the Revolution were written by
participants before the great upheaval had spent its force.
Heated in tone, often intemperate, they were partisan
histories, of dubious value. The contemporaries who
penned them sought less to explain than to praise or damn
the epic disruption which was ripping apart the closely
knit fibers of French life. Everywhere, in France and out,
the Revolution had fervent defenders with eyes for the
good that it was doing; everywhere, too, there were detractors not less vehement than the champions, aghast over
its violence and its rejection of established ways.

Searching their minds for an explanation of what was
happening, men whose lives the Revolution uprooted
tended, while they vigorously denounced its frightfulness,
to discover religious-historical causes for the evil it had
wrought. Human frailty and wickedness, they agreed,
played their part. But to find a fuller explanation of this
cruel attack upon European civilization, writers who were
hostile to the Revolution made much of three forces: the
subversive ideas of the Enlightenment; the conspiracy of
the *philosophes* and their organized followers; and the
workings of providence.

That such explanations gave emotional satisfaction, as
well as solace for material losses, to men whose deepest
sentiments had been outraged, is apparent. As commen-
taries on the origins of the revolutionary movement and
its significance, they had defects which the passage of
time has not lessened. After a century and a half of in-

tensive scholarly research this type of explanation, in an intellectually more sophisticated form, still has a few never-say-die exponents. (*See Reading 1, No. 1.*) One cannot take it seriously. Every facet of the Revolution has been examined in the light of the specialized interest of the investigators. As much as research is capable, it has made that extraordinary explosion of human energies intelligible. What historical investigation has made abundantly clear is that the Revolution was not a conspiracy organized and plotted by purveyors of subversive ideas.

To be sure, the hopes of the future revolutionaries were kindled by ideas. Many young men were under the sway of a kind of prerevolutionary mentality in the years immediately preceding 1789 and immediately following the successful revolutionary activities across the ocean in America. Those activities were widely reported and enthusiastically endorsed. In the broadest sense the ideas by which men were moved held forth the prospect not only of an orderly world, such as France already had, more or less, but also of a world where order for all would be founded upon the liberty of the individual. Not liberty unrestrained and unconfined, but a tempered liberty operating within a newer and different community than the one in which they lived, in a community where there would be equality and rights for its members, where each would work together to advance the happiness and prosperity of all.

These ideas, critical, often mocking, occasionally original, and ever emphatic in stressing liberty of enterprise, of expression and conscience, defended the natural right of the individual together with his fellows to work out his own destiny. They were weapons against the old order, obviously. They did not, however, spring full-grown from the heads of isolated thinkers, linked to one another only by evil intentions; they were conceived in the womb of circumstance. They were the reflection and the products of the historical evolution of the past several generations. They accompanied sustained economic changes which were bringing wealth and power to merchants, manufacturers, and financiers. They attested the expansion of knowledge which had steadily widened the horizon of Europeans, transforming their living habits and secularizing their values. They gave evidence of waning faith in revealed truth and of supreme confidence in science and reason to regenerate the institutions of man.

This pattern of thought and feeling had fashioned itself more markedly in France than anywhere else on the continent of Europe. For in France of the Old Regime, circumstances were most favorable to it. In France, moreover, for two generations and with remarkable effectiveness, writers had expounded and popularized those ideas. Thus the ideas which seemingly made men restive, or even rebellious, were influential because they were related to life and reality, because they propounded satisfactory explanations of why the time was out of joint, because with superb and exaggerated confidence in the power of rational persuasion, their formulators put forth glittering proposals to set it right.

The first group of revolutionists, convinced that there could be no arresting the course of human progress, looked forward to a peaceful transformation of society. Alas, there was to be no easy transition from the bad old regime to a good new regime of freedom, no revolution by persuasion. Ten years later, the out-and-out German conservative, Friedrich von Gentz (whose observations about the Revolution John Quincy Adams translated with approving admiration) could look back and sum it up as an endless offensive without a fixed object, a challenge to almost every human feeling, a torrent purposeless and violent.[1]

So the Revolution then appeared to more than one disillusioned sympathizer, as he saw the men who began it outdistanced by bolder, more radical, and more demanding associates. As new social groups entered in turn upon the stage, new emotions, new grievances and observations were released to mingle with and reenforce the first currents—or to run counter to them. Yet there lay, under the surface of disorder and violence, an inner rhythm of development. It is in war and inflation, class tensions, real and fancied, counter-revolutionary plots and Terror at home, and in a revolutionary crusade against

[1] Friedrich von Gentz, *The French and American Revolutions Compared*. Tr. by J. Q. Adams. Intro. by R. Kirk. (Chicago, 1955).

kings and aristocracies abroad, that one must seek the causes of the successive shocks which troubled the decade.

In 1799 when Bonaparte seized power, the Revolution had sorely disappointed the expectations of many followers. Its heroic proportions, nevertheless, were patent. Whether to admire or lament it, everyone recognized that it had burned its way through the history of France. Within the brief span of ten years, the Revolution effected changes in the status of persons which were nothing short of electrifying. Feudal laws disappeared. In consequence of a colossal transfer of landed property, the Revolution created, for all practical purposes, a nation of small peasant proprietors. Free enterprise in commerce, manufacture, and finance, as well as in things of the spirit, became the order of the day. A secular state, as many Frenchmen had long desired, came into being. Yet revolutionary France did not repudiate its past. The old process of nation-making that Richelieu and Mazarin and Louis XIV had so effectively aided, the Revolution accelerated. Although it was violent and destructive, the Revolution ensured the lasting triumph of powerful forces long working underground in France.

It gave a dramatic fillip, too, to forces embedded in the history of the neighboring states and in states as distant as the newly emancipated United States of America. The revolutionary decade was a stage, a very significant stage, in the development of the entire western world. When word merely of the revolt of the aristocracy became known in 1788, it aroused favorable comment among liberals and progressives outside France, so hostile were men everywhere to French absolutism. But when the Third Estate entered the struggle in 1789 and the unbelievable news spread throughout the world that the Bastille had fallen, the wildest enthusiasm broke loose. The dancing, the demonstrations, and the drinking of the celebrants were native in origin. There was no central world organization to tell Irishmen and Rhinelanders, Americans and Hollanders, that the moment had come for a spontaneous celebration. The political refugees in Paris who in 1789 sent glowing reports to their native lands and the French revolutionaries who in 1792 appealed to the oppressed all over the world, promising them aid in their struggle for liberation, were not conspirators working underground. They made no secret of their intentions: they proudly flaunted their desire to set Europe ablaze.

Revolutionary disturbances swept Holland, Belgium, Switzerland, and northern Italy. In antecedents, in leadership and following, they were independent of each other. Yet they were part of a world movement. Wherever revolutions broke out, they came because governments had forfeited the loyalty of subjects. They came because in those countries, and in Ireland also where revolution failed, men had grievances against the privileged minority. Everywhere, almost without exception, their demand for equality blended with their determination to rid themselves of foreign masters and become independent in their own lands. Native leaders and cautious followers were eager to bring about revolutionary changes provided, however, they did not have to place themselves in too vulnerable a position, provided in short that they could have a revolution under the protective bayonets of the French liberating troops. For that aid they were to pay dearly. For many years the emancipators milked their hosts. Town workers and peasants footed the bill of liberation, too, but no one had to remind them that they were liberated from the Old Regime.

The Revolution outlasted the revolutionary decade. Its ideas and institutions, perpetuated and extended by Napoleon's conquering troops, penetrated deeply into European life. The Revolution as the fulfillment of liberty conquered and converted Europe. It lived on in the consciousness of the hopeful and the disaffected as a passing and unfulfilled promise of equality, as an unforgettable moment in the struggle of democracy against privilege.

— 2 —

THE ANCIEN REGIME AND
THE FAILURE OF REFORM

Economic Progress and Social Change. The France of the Old Regime was a class society grounded in inequality of rights. In law, there were three orders or estates, but out of a total population of between 24 million and 26 million, more than 96 per cent belonged to the Third Estate alone. At most, 500,000 individuals made up the enormously privileged ecclesiastical aristocracy of the first and second estates. In numbers, the secular and regular clergy of 130,000 members was insignificant. Public opinion was sharply critical of the clergy in general, not least of the mode of life of the great prelates. The differences in income, influence, and prestige between the parish clergy, stemming either from the peasantry and the humble town dweller, and the upper clergy of bishops, abbots, and heads of cathedral chapters, who came without exception from the lay nobility, were shocking. The doctrines of the Church, too, were under heavy intellectual fire. The absolute monarchy did not favor too close relations between the clergy and Rome.

Nevertheless, the clergy possessed influence far beyond its numbers. The Church was an organized body, a self-governing corporate structure, hierarchically arranged and subject to firm internal discipline. It was almost a state within a state, with its own officers of administration, its own courts of law, and a representative assembly meeting at stated intervals for, among other purposes, regulating its relations with the monarchy. The Church was immensely wealthy, enjoying great income from the annual revenue on its vast landed possessions, from the tithe that it levied on all crops, and from many gifts and fees. It was powerful as well as influential, holding a monopoly of the registration of births, deaths, and marriages. It controlled poor relief and education. Sharing with the state in the censorship of all publications and upholding the traditions and the values of the established order, the Church was a profoundly conservative force, a pillar of society.

The number of individuals making up the lay aristocracy of the nobility, which was the second order, has been estimated at between 100,000 and 400,000, or between one and three per cent of the total population. Unlike the clergy, it was not corporatively organized. But as a legally distinct social group it was set apart from all others by its own rights and privileges. Among them were the rights enjoyed by its members to be tried at special courts, to be exempted from the heaviest of the direct taxes, and to be granted preferential rates for the others; to have a monopoly of the highest positions in the civil administration and in the Church and, in the closing years of the Old Regime, in the military, naval, and diplomatic services as well.

This aristocracy was set apart also by virtue of its wealth, which consisted mainly though not exclusively of feudal land and urban real estate. As was true of the clergy, there were striking variations among its members in respect to wealth, influence, and manner of life. There was an old nobility of military or presumed military origin, a few of whom lived in conspicuous extravagance at Versailles while most of them vegetated in inconspicuous want on their impoverished country estates. There was also a nobility of more recent origin. Recruited from the wealthy upper middle class, its members had obtained noble status through the purchase of patents of nobility, through intermarriage or, most frequently of all, through the purchase of offices in the administration which automatically carried nobility with them. The leading figures of this aristocracy swelled their wealth and influence by lucrative investments in business enterprises or in large-scale agriculture. From the ranks of the magistrates in the superior courts, the *parlements,* came the tough opponents of the absolute monarchy, the *parlementaires,* who time and again during the century obstructed royal policy and challenged the very theory of absolutism. Cultivated and refined, rich and arrogant too, they spearheaded the revival of the influence and power of the eighteenth-century nobility.

The overwhelming majority of the population belonged to the Third Estate. This was a legal catch-all in which the middle class, or the *bourgeoisie*, to use the French term, was the most important segment. There were layers, too, within the bourgeoisie which made up 10 to 12 per cent of the population and perhaps half of the population of the towns and cities. There was an upper bourgeoisie composed principally of the wealthy new business elite and government officials not of the nobility. There was a middle bourgeoisie, comprising independent craftsmen and artisans, well-to-do merchants and traders, booksellers and printers, members of the rapidly growing liberal professions: writers, scholars, and lawyers. While all other town dwellers technically constituted the populace (*gens du peuple*), it was difficult in practice to distinguish between representatives of the working class proper, such as journeymen, apprentices, clerks, and domestics, and the members of the petty bourgeoisie of small shopkeepers and neighborhood tradesmen.

For those with some capital the times were good during the greater part of the eighteenth century. International trade was booming in volume and value. On the eve of the Revolution, the value of the total foreign trade was slightly above 1,000,000,000 livres, most of it in the staple colonial products of raw cotton, sugar, tobacco, coffee, tea, chocolate, and Negro slaves. In consequence of the great profits, a new plutocracy of merchants and financiers established itself along the Atlantic and Mediterranean seaboards, investing and reinvesting their gains in refining and processing plants, in financial and insurance operations, and in advanced forms of industrial enterprise. The unprecedented increase of 3,000,000 in population since mid-century helped their cause, furnishing them with both a new labor force and a broader market, while an equally stupendous increase in the amount of minted money in circulation—between 2,000,000,000 and 3,000,000,000 livres in gold and silver—elevated sales prices by 50 per cent.

The boom was great but guild rules and restrictions, governmental monopolies and controls, internal customs dues, a multiplicity of weights and measures, contradictory legal practices and principles, all those obstacles seriously impeded economic growth and retarded economic unification. Moreover, this expansionist cycle brought to the workers few benefits other than increased employment opportunities. In terms of purchasing power, their real wages were lower at the end of the long cycle than they had been at the start, for while real prices went up on an average by about 45 per cent, real wages rose only by about 22 per cent. When the boom ended in the seventies, and a recession set in, the hardship of the working people was appalling.

Nor was the expansionist period an unmitigated blessing for the peasantry. France, it must be remembered, was overwhelmingly rural and the status of the French peasantry was unique, unparalleled in Europe. Nearly all peasants were legally free and perhaps three out of every four heads of families were proprietors, in fact if not in title, of the land that they cultivated. Subject to the payment of manorial dues and services, they were free to bequeath, inherit, and improve if they could, the plot that they worked. What they owned as a group made up close to 40 per cent of the arable land. Nevertheless, the total was not nearly enough for the needs of a rapidly growing population.

The average plot was grossly inadequate. Thus, the majority of the peasants also *worked* a large part of the remaining cultivable soil which they did not own but which was owned either by the monarchy, the Church, the lay aristocracy, or the bourgeoisie. If they were fortunate, they worked this additional land as tenant farmers; if not, as sharecroppers. Apart from a tiny minority that was well off, most peasants only managed somehow, by pooling the combined labor force of the family with such income from supplementary work as they could find, to make do in good times. One out of every four families, if not more, was completely landless. For the heads of such families, the alternative to disaster was to hire themselves out as farmhands or do piecework as spinners or weavers for the town entrepreneur. Even in good times, the highways of France swarmed with tramps and beggars; and when times were hard, with brigands too.

Illiteracy was general among them. For the average peasant, his small piece of land was insufficient. He had no capital to fall back on. His obligations to state, Church, and lord of the manor were many and heavy. Unaided, he could not improve his lot. The Physiocrats, the great capitalist agricultural reformers, pressed their campaign to improve and increase agricultural production, but the changes which they advocated decreased the poor peasants' margin of security. Enclosure of their plots, abolition of their ancient collective rights to the common fields, division of cleared or reclaimed land, higher rentals for improved land, all these improvements were burdens rather than blessings for peasants who could not take advantage of the new opportunities.

Beginning with about 1776, trial after trial afflicted the rural population. Reversing the trend since the early decades of the century, grain prices sagged. This gradual decline continued until 1788, when the harvest failed, which shot grain prices to a century high. A very small minority of the peasants benefitted from these developments, but most did not. The greater number had to pay the high market prices for their seed as well as for their bread. Meantime, landlords, themselves affected by rising costs, had raised the rentals on leased land. In this same span of years the important wine production segment of rural economy was suffering from a glutted market and collapsing prices. Thus the income of many peasants was dropping off sharply, just when for all of them grain and bread prices were soaring. To cap the climax of misfortune, the boom burst in industrial expansion, most of all in textile production, and a severe crisis of unemployment followed.

The winter of 1788-1789 tried the fortitude of the poor. It was the coldest in the memory of living men. Provisions were inadequate, naturally, for relief and no public works program existed to take care of the needy. In the towns there was rioting for bread, work, and living wages; in the countryside, half-starved peasants were on the loose. The cry, to be heard again during the Revolution, that "the brigands" were coming, reverberated throughout the land. The military authorities had been called out more than once before this to break up demonstrations for higher wages and better work conditions. Now in this crisis of unexampled intensity, both economic and political, the people had no one to turn to for guidance and leadership save their bourgeois associates.

The Creed of the Bourgeoisie. The outlook of the upper middle classes was rationalist, experimental, humanitarian, and utilitarian. The procedures and the conclusions of the great scientific innovators of the last two centuries gave it its texture. Confidence in the ability of man to change things for the better was the heart of it. It was an outlook which corresponded with, indeed depended upon and reflected, the dynamic economic developments of the century. Into it entered the high hopes of the followers of Descartes and into it streamed the currents of Dutch and English thought. This belief in the possibility of achieving orderliness in the world of human relations, which was also presumably governed, like the physical universe, by "the laws of nature and of nature's God," was a new ideology. It was a species of religious conviction, the secularized faith of a new social and economic elite whose concern was largely with the here and now. It was the creed of men who had the means to investigate, ponder, and discuss the phenomena of the world in which they lived; who had, too, the emotional predisposition, because of their grievances and thwarted political ambition, to accept the newer conceptions of government, religion, ethics, economic practices, and social relationships. (*See Reading 1, No. II.*)

The writers who pieced together the parts of their creed and gave it a definite form called themselves, with perhaps an allowable absence of modesty, "philosophers" (*les philosophes*). In countless works, all of them lucid and persuasive—for they all were expositors of talent—and some of them passionately eloquent, they condemned the abuses of the Old Regime, sparing neither institutions nor rooted beliefs. They employed their literary skill mainly to condemn, but from their pens there also flowed a stream of dazzling projects for improvement. They dangled before men the prospects of a world where freedom and equality of opportunity would prevail, where fresh creative human energies would be released so that men could think, believe, work, prosper, aid their fellows, and be happy.

What they said, they said openly, and often they paid heavily for their boldness. They were neither sect nor organized group. Their activities spanned two generations. They stressed different aspects of a common endeavor, depending upon their interests and competence. If the *philosophes* were influential, it was in part because they believed in full sincerity that they were speaking for all mankind. If their readers were responsive, it was because they accepted those claims. In the *philosophes'* campaign against ignorance and stupidity, dirt and disease, cruel laws and slavery, war and militarism, they were in effect saying that above all nations was humanity.

They were influential too for a reason which was distinct from the intrinsic merit of their works. Intermittently for almost four decades, from about 1748 to 1788, in order to counterbalance the *parlementaires,* the monarchy cast a tolerant eye upon their writings. In those years, the new gospel was spread along the improved roads and canals, in old salons and new discussion clubs, in schools, provincial academies, in town cafes and in the marketplace, that here on earth man could attain peace, security, and happiness. The political reforms that the *philosophes* advocated, like their fiscal reforms and their defense of free intellectual enterprise, were directed to people already sufficiently instructed and well-off to be able to aspire for still greater advantages. Neither radicals nor democrats, they feared the populace, the *canaille,* as it was called in France, or the "swinish multitude," as Burke described it in England. Their understanding of the world of the propertyless and uneducated, who could not conceivably rise to a higher station, was the least of their virtues.

The Failure of Reform. The reform movement for which the *philosophes* supplied the blueprints went back to the years immediately following the close of the Seven Years' War (1763). With disciples of Physiocrats installed in the administration, the campaign began for agricultural improvements, free internal grain trade, liberalized trading relations abroad, and industrial production released from state controls and guild restrictions.

The counterpart to this program of economic reform was the effort of the monarchy to put its administrative house in order. Superficially, the system of central administration as it had finally evolved during the reign of Louis XIV seemed orderly enough. Actually it functioned badly, with overlapping jurisdictions and ministerial rivalries. There was neither leadership from the king nor guidance from a prime minister to initiate policy. The regional administration also lacked uniformity. In provinces which had been incorporated early in France's history (*pays d'élections*) the authority of the intendant of justice, taxes, and finance was virtually uncontested. In the newer provinces (*pays d'états*) this representative of the Crown was in no sense an agent of "ministerial despotism," for he was at all turns hampered and obstructed by the local vested interests.

The administration of civil justice was weak. Many of the law officers were staggeringly incompetent when not also corrupt. Legal principles concerning persons and property varied from area to area. In all the myriad courts which covered the country—royal, ecclesiastical, manorial —procedure was slow and costly. Often it was cumbersome, frequently dishonest. As for the barbarous procedure of criminal justice, it was shocking to the humanitarian consciousness of the age. The taxation system, too, was the product of historical growth and reflected social and economic evolution. The most crushing direct taxes were levied on the peasantry, while the upper classes enjoyed partial or total exemption. There were also burdensome indirect taxes which were given out under contract for collection. Of these, the *gabelle,* or the tax on the sale of salt, which was a government monopoly, was the most onerous, unjust and hated. There were outrageous variations in price, which ranged from thirteen sous a pound in many regions to only one sou elsewhere, and there were the sharpest differences in the amount that householders were compelled by law to purchase per annum. In consequence, smuggling was rampant, and between the smugglers and the government there was an undeclared war.

No other aspect of the Old Regime was so severely criticized as the fiscal system, but it remained unchanged to the end.

The annual revenue of the monarchy was not adequate for its needs. Year by year the deficit grew larger, as did the standing debt. Court wastefulness and extravagance, increased costs, and new administrative responsibilities accounted for part of the deficit, but it was the high cost of war which pushed the government down the road of bankruptcy. All the great wars of the century had been financed by borrowing. When France looked at the bill for its aid to the American colonists, the ministers found that almost 2,000,000,000 additional livres had been added to the earlier total. All told the state debt in 1788 amounted to more than 4,500,000,000 livres, on which the annual interest charges were 318,000,000 livres. In the last fiscal year of 1788-1789, the budget was more unbalanced than ever: income was estimated at 560,000,000 livres, while expenditures were calculated at 630,000,000. In addition to the 318,000,000 livres earmarked for interest charges, an additional 165,000,000 were set aside for current defense. More than 75 per cent of the total expenditures went for the military budget alone, an eloquent commentary on the government's desperate need for increased revenue.

Breakdown of the Administrative System. It was thus not defects beyond repair that made the administrative system break down when it did, nor yet the frivolous indifference of Louis XV or the weakness of Louis XVI. The governing system broke down because it was subjected simultaneously between 1787 and 1789 to the extraordinary strain of three related crises—political, financial, and economic; because the reforming ministers lacked time and sufficient support for their projects; because, finally, the *privilégiés* willed that the reforms, which would have made the absolute monarchy viable, should fail.

From 1715 on, the judicial aristocracy of the parlements had used their right to make representations (*remontrances*) concerning proposed legislation, as well as their right to register new laws, as a club against the monarchy. For decades they took the stand that they were defending "the fundamental laws" of France against the arbitrary will of the king and his ministers. In 1757 they took advantage of the government's embarrassment during the Seven Years' War to advance the claim that their jurisdiction applied not merely to procedure in law-making, but also applied to the substance of all legislation. (*See Reading 2, No. I.*) Finally, they elaborated the challenging doctrine that all the parlements of France were actually parts of a single organic body possessing the constitutional right to speak in the name of the nation. Louis XV was sufficiently aroused (1766) from his lethargy to rebuke the claimants to his authority in the most scorching declaration of royal absolutism that the century heard. (*See Reading 2, No. II.*)

The Crown did not follow up this move and crush its opponents once and for all. It missed its opportunity when Chancellor Maupeou abolished the parlement of Paris outright in 1770 and set up a new court with restricted territorial jurisdiction and without the right to make remonstrances. For four years, from 1770 to 1774, the *parlementaires* fought back, rallying their numerous followers to their support with a propaganda campaign that threw the country into turmoil. When the young Louis XVI mounted the throne in 1774, he was advised by his experienced counselors to win popularity by restoring the parlements. This he did, with sad results, for if the noisy demonstrations of joy all over France and the Te Deums that were sung had any meaning, they signified that the prestige of the monarchy was visibly declining.

The discrediting of the government's authority continued after this reversal. When Louis XVI appointed a number of notable reformers to the ministry, particularly the famous Turgot, a veteran intendant and champion of physiocratic reform, to the key post of Controller-General of Finances, Turgot's bourgeois admirers were jubilant. But they rejoiced too soon, for the *privilégiés* soon paralyzed his activities. His edict establishing free internal grain trade was rescinded while he was still in office; Louis XVI at first compelled the parlements to register Turgot's edicts suppressing the guilds and the compulsory road service of the peasantry (*see Reading 3, Nos. I, II*), but he soon yielded to pressure and dismissed his reforming minister. The guilds were restored and the aristocracy had won another round (1776).

Worsening of the Financial Crisis. In the ten years which followed, the financial crisis grew worse; for those were the years of financial aid to the American colonists. The "wizard" of finance, the famous Swiss banking expert, Jacques Necker, could not solve the problem when he was in charge of financial affairs from 1776 to 1781. From 1783 to 1787 it was an experienced, intelligent, and highly resourceful intendant, Calonne, who held the office of Controller-General. For several years he made a valiant effort to broaden the base for additional revenue by a program of government aid to production and trade. When the heavy debts that he had contracted fell due, he, too, turned reformer. In a secret memorandum to Louis XVI late in 1786, he outlined a comprehensive reform program that included most of the recommendations already made by Turgot and Necker. Only too aware that the parlements would not register his proposed edicts, Calonne hit upon the idea of calling an Assembly of Notables whose members he himself would carefully select in advance to insure a rubber-stamp approval of his proposal. The idea was ingenious, but the move proved a blunder. In referring the decision to the Notables, he appealed from the formal constitutional opposition of the parlements to the informal resistance of other equally staunch conservatives. The final crisis of the Old Regime began when the first Assembly of Notables met in the spring of 1787.

FROM ARISTOCRATIC REVOLT TO BOURGEOIS REVOLUTION, 1787-1789

The Aristocracy Overplays Its Hand. Calonne had miscalculated. After six weeks, the opposition of the Notables proved too strong and Louis XVI dropped the minister whose outlook was broad but whose tactics were vulnerable. (*See Reading 4, No. 1.*) Six additional weeks of deadlock convinced his successor, Loménie de Brienne, who had been Calonne's foremost critic in the Notables, that nothing was to be gained through that body. On his advice the king dismissed them, leaving Brienne with no other recourse than to try his fortunes with the parlement of Paris. Parlement balked, however, at the new land tax and higher stamp fees on official transactions, and in rejecting them it declared openly that only the Estates General had the power to make permanent changes in the tax structure. That statement read well, as if it were a defense of the principle of no taxation without representation. What the *parlementaires* actually meant was that in an Estates General dominated by the aristocracy, no changes would be made in the existing tax structure. Louis XVI held a *lit de justice* (so called because the king sat upon a bed or divan when attending meetings of the parlement) to compel them to register the taxes, but on the following day parlement solemnly declared the registration illegal and null.

Their opposition forced Brienne to drop the new tax proposals. Since the receipts, however, from some emergency taxes which parlement had extended, were insufficient to meet pressing short-term obligations, in November of that same year, Brienne appealed to it to register fresh loans and thus tide the government over. With supreme self-confidence, the magistrates turned him down, scorning his *quid pro quo* to summon the Estates General within five years. Again the king's fiat forced parlement to register his minister's measure; and again, and more boldly, the parlement protested, demanding this time that he summon the Estates General immediately. The struggle now widened, for in the following half year the magistrates challenged the very concept of monarchical absolutism. In a notable remonstrance the parlement of Paris, joined by the local parlements, flatly accused the monarch of substituting arbitrary despotism for the fundamental laws. (*See Reading 4, No. II A.*) This was open defiance, rebellion.

In this intolerable atmosphere the Crown quietly took steps to crush the parlements once and for all. The preparations were disclosed and to ward off the blow, the magistrates issued a declaration proclaiming themselves the guardians of the fundamental laws of France. While not wholly valid, that declaration was clearly designed to embarrass the government and win public support. The expected action came on May 8, 1788, when an edict, called the Lamoignon Edict after its formulator, the chancellor of the realm, deprived the parlements of the right to register royal edicts, and established a new court for that purpose, whose members were to be appointed and paid by the government. The suspended magistrates hit back, organizing virtual revolts against the ruling. The king would not steel himself to use the military and Brienne's warnings were greeted with jeers. The aristocratic revolt was making headway.

At this point the monarchy tacked in the wind, taking in sail. Early in July (1788), after announcing that the Estates General would be assembled in the following year, it appealed to all interested persons for information. The appeal was a maneuver to broaden the controversy and get the bourgeoisie into the struggle as a counterweight to the *parlementaires*. Pamphlets by the hundreds were soon written and circulated in response to the appeal. The move was clever, but unfortunately for the government it released a chain reaction which could not be controlled. Both magistrates and bourgeois leaders got out of hand.

When Necker began his second term as financial minister, he restored the *parlementaires* to their offices, judging it good tactics to tolerate them until the government would be strong enough to curb them. Once in office again, however, they surpassed themselves in arrogance or perhaps merely in overestimating their strength and popularity. On September 25, only two days after they resumed their duties, they formally demanded that the Estates General "be regularly convoked and composed . . . in accordance with the forms observed in 1614." As the Estates General had not met for 175 years since 1614, this demand served public notice that the parlements intended to disregard almost two centuries of change.

Their popularity collapsed overnight; and their associates in the struggle against royal absolutism, the "Nationals" or the "Patriots" as the bourgeois leaders called themselves, broke away. Joined by a handful of sympathizers from the liberal wing of the *parlementaires,* they formed a somewhat mysterious steering committee, the Committee of Thirty, and organized for political action. As 1788 drew to a close, it was apparent that the "Aristos" had overreached themselves: they had simultaneously undermined the monarchy on which they were dependent for their privileges and aroused the commoners to whom their privileges were abhorrent.

The Elections to the Estates General.   The Patriots organized an electoral campaign, which had two principal aims. The first was to "double the Third," in other words to have the number of deputies of the Third Estate equal the combined total of the deputies of the first two orders. They also demanded that the meetings be held in common rather than by separate delegations and that the voting be by head instead of by order or estate. If the voting were to be by estate, the likelihood was great that the two privileged orders would side with each other and outvote the Third Estate two to one; if the voting were in common the advantage of numbers would lie with the latter. They counted on a favorable ruling to that end from the Royal Council, where Necker was friendly to them. Necker, however, was thoroughly conscious of the strong opposition in the Council, so he emulated Calonne and called an Assembly of Notables, hoping to bypass his colleagues.

Unfortunately, the Notables turned him down, as they had Calonne, while at the same time the princes of the blood (excepting the Duke of Orleans and the Count of Provence) drafted a protest against what they considered the subversive tenor of the pamphlets which were flooding the country. (*See Reading 4, No. II B.*) The popular hue and cry against these developments strengthened Necker's hand and by a bare majority the Council agreed to the "doubling." That decision was published at the end of 1788 under the curious title, *Result of the Council,* which carried the implication that the king personally did not approve it. Moreover, since the Council remained divided on the vital point of whether the voting would be by order or in common, the language of the *Result of the Council* was deliberately ambiguous. (*See Reading 4, No. III.*)

Once again disorder flared up, largely over the disputed interpretation of the *Result*. In that setting the most influential of all the many pamphlets was published, the famous *What Is the Third Estate?* of Abbé Sieyès. Sieyès advanced two profoundly revolutionary theses: (1) the identification of the nation exclusively with the Third Estate: "Take away the privileged orders and the nation is not smaller but greater"; and (2) the contention that the nation or Third Estate alone had constituent power, *i.e.,* the power to give France a constitution. (*See Reading 5, No. I.*) His argument was the direct reply to the doctrine of the *parlementaires* that France already had a constitution embedded in its history and entrusted to them for safekeeping.

Millions of Frenchmen went to the polls early in 1789. The electoral procedure was simple for the first two orders who voted directly for their deputies. It was more complicated for the Third Estate but also very liberal. Virtually all men of the age of twenty-five and over, whose names were inscribed on the tax rolls, were given the right to vote. But the elections were indirect, ranging from two stages in the country to three or four in the towns and cities. In the earliest and intermediate stages of the elections the rural voters greatly outnumbered the townspeople, but in the final stage, largely because of their sense of inferiority, the numerically superior peasant delegates voted for bourgeois deputies to represent them at

Versailles. All told, 1,201 deputies, without counting alternates, were elected: 300 for the clergy, 291 for the nobility, and 610 for the Third Estate. The overwhelming majority of the representatives of the clergy were parish priests—only 46 prelates were elected—whose sympathies lay with the commoners. On the other hand, most of the deputies of the nobility were country noblemen, traditionalist and conservative in their outlook. There was, nevertheless, a large liberal minority of ninety, many of whom had been across the seas to aid the Americans in their Revolution.

In the main the deputies of the Third Estate—the Commons as they were to call themselves—came from the liberal professions, bringing with them already established reputations to Versailles. Authentic spokesmen of rural France were not elected. Many of these bourgeois deputies were lawyers, undoubtedly too many from the point of view of a balanced representation of a France that was so overwhelmingly peasant in composition. Bailly, the astronomer, was one of the Commons, as well as Target, the distinguished jurist. Besides Barnave and Mounier, already known for their defiance of the monarch in 1788, there were also two deputies already famous who were not from the Third Estate but were elected to represent it: the oracular Abbé Sieyès and the Count of Mirabeau, colorful, dynamic, and well-informed. Not yet famous, though soon to be so, were the two young lawyers, Maximilien Robespierre and Jacques Danton.

The Cahiers.   At each stage of the elections, where there was more than one stage, the voters had drawn up *cahiers,* or lists of grievances and suggestions. It was the general cahier for each large electoral unit of the Third Estate that the deputies took with them to the Estates General, but it was in the tens of thousands of local or primary cahiers that the wishes of the peasants, petty bourgeoisie, and workers were recorded, detailed demands which were rarely included in the composite final text. *(See Reading 5, No. II A, B.)*

The area of agreement between the general cahiers was striking. Far from attacking the hereditary monarchy or the Church, nearly all the cahiers abounded in expressions of loyalty and respect for those two great forces which had molded France. They called for a written declaration to guarantee the civil rights of the individual. All of them recognized the sanctity of property rights. Agreement was general, too, that royal and ministerial "despotism" should be ended and local and regional elected assemblies should ensure effective administrative decentralization. Despite the view of the *parlementaires* to the contrary, it was also generally agreed that France was to have a written constitution and an elected representative assembly, meeting periodically, with control over taxation. Taxation was to be proportionately equal for all subjects.

There were also sharp divergences between the cahiers of the different estates. Where the middle-class cahiers stressed "liberty," the cahiers of the nobility emphasized the traditional "liberties," meaning their feudal rights and honorific privileges. The nobles also intended that control of the new or restored assemblies should rest in their hands. Within their broad acceptance of the principle of tax equality, they still asked that special treatment be given to their members. The cahiers of the clergy, too, frequently disagreed with those of the Third Estate. Many wished to limit full freedom of press and publication. Many opposed toleration for "heretics," namely Protestants, Jews, and deists. They wished to maintain the corporate structure of the clergy together with church control over education, poor relief, and the register of births, marriages, and deaths.

Between the estates, then, there were important areas of disagreement; and within each estate there were divergences and potential hostility. Yet hopes ran high for the "regeneration" of France, as in the early spring of 1789 the deputies made their way to Versailles.

The June Days.   The formal opening session on May 5 threw cold water on the hopes of the Commons. The king himself spoke briefly and, so it seemed to many, beside the point. Speaking for the government, Barentin, the reactionary Keeper of the Seals, made it clear that the Crown would not consider voting in common unless such procedure were supported by the Estates General as a whole. In short, if the monarchy had its way, there would be no voting in common. Necker, on the other

hand, recommended that voting by order be kept pro-
v'sionally, a recommendation which carried the implica-
ion that it might later be given up. All that was confusing enough, but Necker scarcely touched on the most
important subject of all, the question of constitutional
reforms. Thus, the privileged orders did not know what
the limits of change would be, and the Third Estate
whether there would even be a beginning.

Consequently, a crisis ensued when the king commanded each order to verify its own credentials and to
organize itself as a separate body. If the Third Estate
assented, all hope of voting by head in the future seemed
forlorn, if not utterly hopeless. If it did not, it would
place itself in the position of defying the monarch. The
Commons had not come to Versailles to renounce reforms. Yet they were too loyal to defy Louis XVI openly.
They thereupon adopted delaying tactics. For five weeks,
while conducting a masterly campaign of not verifying
credentials independently, they carried on active negotiations with the other orders. In this way a month went by
with little gained and much lost. The reservoir of hope,
good will, and patience was slowly being eroded.

On June 10, the Paris delegation of Third Estate
deputies took their seats. Under the inspiration of Abbé
Sieyès and in accordance with his contention that the
Third Estate was the nation, his fellow deputies issued a
final "invitation" to the other two orders to verify credentials in common as representatives of the nation. On
the 12th, they began to take the roll call. The nobility
ignored these meetings completely; a minority of the
clergy were present. By June 17, the verification of credentials was completed, and the Commons, by a vote of
491 to 89, solemnly proclaimed themselves the National
Assembly. Without royal assent and going far beyond
their instructions, the deputies of the Third Estate had
assumed national sovereignty. This was the first act of
the Revolution. (*See Reading 6, No. I.*)

Conservatives at once brought heavy pressure upon
the king to use force against the rebels, but he agreed to
Necker's proposal that a Royal Session be called to draft
compromise terms on which the struggle could be ended.
Accordingly, the king gave orders to close the hall in

which the Commons had been meeting in order to have necessary alterations made in seating capacity to accommodate the deputies of all three orders. When, on the 20th, the Commons found themselves locked out, they jumped to the conclusion that Louis was planning to dissolve the National Assembly. In the circumstances, that misunderstanding, if misunderstanding it was, was natural. Had Louis XVI been more resolute there would have been less uncertainty over his intentions. While some of the frightened and indignant deputies were for adjourning to the friendlier setting of Paris, cooler counsel ultimately prevailed. It was only a short walk from the barred hall to a large indoor tennis court used by the court aristocracy. There, the embattled Commons took their celebrated oath "never to separate . . . until the Constitution of the kingdom was established and affirmed upon a solid basis." (*See Reading 6, No. II.*) All but one deputy subscribed to this formal and dramatic act of defiance.

The issue now was squarely up to Louis XVI, who could meet no issue squarely. Wavering and uncertain, he finally accepted the decision of the Royal Council where, after angry and prolonged discussions, Necker's conciliatory proposals had been turned down. Instead, approval had been given to Barentin's fateful motion that at the Royal Session the government would declare the proceedings of June 17 null and void; that a show of force should be made to overawe the deputies; and that the future organization of the Estates General would be discussed by the separate orders.

Accordingly, heavy detachments of loyal troops surrounded the meeting hall on the morning of the 23rd. All nondeputies were excluded from the galleries. Necker's seat was ominously vacant, for he had made up his mind to resign in protest. Barentin spoke for the government. It was the royal will, he announced, to have the ancient distinctions of the three orders maintained. The proceedings of June 17 as well as those which followed were illegal and unconstitutional. In future, while matters of general interest would be discussed in common, constitutional reorganization would be taken up separately by each of the three orders, as would discussion of feudal and manorial rights and the prerogatives of the nobility.

Then Barentin submitted the royal legislative program. On May 5, that declaration of intentions would have made a good point of departure. On June 23, it came exactly seven weeks too late. The Commons had gone well beyond it. Too late and too provocative also were Louis XVI's open hints that he was now directing policy—"It is I at present who am doing everything for the happiness of my people"—as well as his command that the deputies leave the Salle des Menus Plaisirs and proceed on the following day to designated meeting halls set aside for each order. (*See Reading 6, No. III.*)

The deputies of the privileged orders followed Louis XVI when he left the hall. The Commons remained, defiant and magnificent in their courage: "We are today what we were yesterday," was Abbé Sieyès' laconic response to the command, while Mirabeau thundered that only the force of bayonets could expel them. Again it was up to the king; and again Louis XVI could not or would not brace himself to use bayonets. The troops returned to their barracks. The Commons reaffirmed the decrees of June 17 and proclaimed that their members were free from arrest.

In the course of the next few days deputies from the clergy and nobility drifted over to the Commons. By the 27th, 830 deputies were attending the meetings of the National Assembly, with only a minority of 371 abstaining. At this point, word came to the king that a crowd of 30,000 Parisians was making ready to move on the palace in Versailles unless he compelled the abstainers to join the majority. Yielding to fear, he gave the order. The struggle was ended and the king, so it appeared, had given in to the bourgeois revolutionists. In reality Louis had only bent before the storm. First he gave orders that six regiments of troops move up to Versailles. Then he summoned ten additional regiments of foreign mercenaries to take up their stations in and around Paris. By early July it was evident that military force would decide the future of a revolution which, save for the king's weakness and vacillation, might have developed without violence.

— 4 —

NEW FRANCE, 1789-1792

The End of the Old Regime, July-October 1789.
When word spread that the troops had come and Necker
had been dismissed, consternation gripped Versailles and
Paris. The deputies, fearing that the soldiers would dissolve the assembly by force, sent delegations to the king
to protest. The Paris working classes and petty bourgeoisie were afraid that the soldiery would suppress their
demonstrations and take vengeance on them for their
part in the agitation against soaring food prices and unemployment. More prosperous Parisians feared both the
troops and the restive, propertyless Paris populace, but
they feared even more the vagrants, beggars, "brigands,"
and other rootless wanderers whom cold, hunger, and
unemployment had driven into the city. Since the police
force and the French Guard of the regular army in
Paris were sympathetic to the demonstrators, representative Paris businessmen organized their own guard (*milice
bourgeoise*) to protect life and property. They also took
over political control by setting up an emergency municipal administration.

On the morning of July 14, a milling crowd, mostly of
small guildmasters and workers joined by the vagrants
and reinforced later in the day by soldiers from the
mutinous French Guard, turned up before the gates of
the Bastille. Rumor had spread that arms and ammunition
were plentiful in that formidable old fortress which was
still occasionally used as a state prison. The crowd negotiated with the governor to withdraw his cannon from
the embrasures, which he did, and to surrender the
citadel, which he refused to do. Negotiations broke down
when the garrison troops through panic or misunderstand-

ing fired upon the demonstrators who had penetrated into
the outer court. The crowd then lay siege to the fortress
and, toward evening, the French Guard. which had
dragged small cannon through the city, carried it by storm.
The assault was not primarily to liberate the prisoners—
there were in fact only seven of them at the time—but to
get arms; and the victory was sullied by cruel reprisals.
Nevertheless, the Bastille was a symbol of despotism and
the besiegers had suffered heavily to capture it, 150 of
them lying dead or wounded. As the intoxicating news
spread that the Bastille had fallen, the will to believe improved upon the literal truth. The legend was born that
a heroic, freedom-loving people had risen in their might
against despotism.

So far as its momentous consequences were concerned,
the capture of the Bastille did save the assembly, now
officially known as the National Constituent Assembly.
Louis XVI recalled Necker and sent away the troops. He
made a ceremonial trip to Paris, as though to symbolize
his acceptance of the insurrection (*see Reading 7, No. 1
A*) and recognized the new municipal government, called
the Commune of Paris. Revolutionists rejoiced as all over
France new communes replaced the old oligarchic municipalities and units of the "National Guard," the former
bourgeois militia, were set up. The celebrated La Fayette
was named commander of the Guard in Paris. Revolutionists rejoiced, but many "Aristos," thoroughly frightened
by the pace of change, fled the country, the first of
several contingents of émigrés.

While this was happening, violence raged in the countryside. The peasantry had been on the move since early
spring, but in the last weeks of July, as reports began
to circulate that the fleeing "Aristos" were inciting "brigands" to attack the peasants, a panic fear, "The Great
Fear," swept over most of France. This *Grande Peur*
was ultimately to subside, but not until the peasants,
armed against nonexistent brigands, had turned their
weapons against the very real and very hated lords and
their bailiffs. They stormed the manor houses and burned
the records of their obligations, and no authorities at
first could hold them in check. The old intendants and
their aides had fled or had been driven away; the old

law courts were suspended; the police and gendarmerie took no action.

When this appalling news reached Versailles, many deputies immediately clamored for vigorous repression. The more farsighted realized that repression alone without meeting peasant grievances would not suffice. So at a caucus of liberal deputies it was agreed that at the next session, one of them would move that the personal obligations of peasants be abolished outright, while the dues deriving from property rights would be abolished subject to compensation for the landlord. This was a calculated maneuver to end peasant disorder. Whatever its merits, the planners lost control over their colleagues during the famous night session of August fourth. In an atmosphere of mounting and almost indescribable emotionalism, deputy after deputy took the floor to give up traditional rights and privileges. Before the session adjourned at two o'clock on the following morning, the exhausted but happy deputies had legislated the Old Regime out of existence. (*See Reading 7, No. I B.*)

The subsequent revision of the August 4 decrees safeguarded property rights according to the original intentions, but the definitive formulation did not restore the privileges which had been renounced during the sacrificial frenzy. The tithe remained abolished without compensation. Exclusive hunting and fishing rights, as well as rights of manorial justice, went by the board. Personal tax privileges were given up; all citizens became eligible for public office. Not only personal privileges were swept aside, but also municipal, corporate and provincial prerogatives. The Old Regime was to be no more as the new French nation came into being. Henceforth, there were no more lords, prelates or commoners, only Frenchmen. Brittany and Burgundy, Provence and Dauphiny, gave up their separate statehood; there was only "the nation," France.

As the communes and the detachments of the local National Guard were restoring order in the countryside, the deputies felt free to go on with their reconstruction of France. On August 26, they laid the foundation of the new regime by voting the famous Declaration of the Rights of Man and the Citizen. (*See Reading 7, No. I C.*)

While drawing heavily upon English and American ideas and charters, the Declaration was most realistically attuned to the historic experiences of living Frenchmen. The first article proclaimed that men were born and remained free and equal in rights; and this great charter of human rights specifically enumerated the equalities that Frenchmen treasured most: equality before the law; equality of taxation; and equal rights to public employment.

The natural rights of man the Declaration defined as liberty, property, security, and resistance to oppression. In protest against the practices of royal absolutism and the claims of the parlements, the Declaration transferred sovereignty to the entire nation. Sovereignty resided in the nation; only law could limit the exercise of men's rights; and law was the expression of the general will in the formation of which all citizens could partake.

There was no elaboration upon the statement that property rights were sacred, because all men took it for granted. Freedom of trade and industry were not defined in detail, because that, too, seemed axiomatic. On the other hand, the charter did not include rights of assembly, petition, and association; nor the rights to work, of public assistance, and instruction. Only a few of the cahiers had raised those demands. Liberty of thought and expression was specifically recognized, but its exercise was made subject to responsibility for its abuse. So far as religious freedom was concerned, the Declaration did not go beyond enjoining tolerance.

By what it omitted then, as well as by what it.underscored, the Declaration was designed for French needs. Nevertheless, its appeal was to be universal. There was nothing in it explicitly to rule out the possibility that property rights and free economic enterprise should be restricted or that political rights be more democratically extended.

After the passage of those decrees and the restoration of order in the provinces, France began to settle down. By his vacillation and his double-dealing, however, Louis XVI again precipitated a crisis. It was doubtless the beginning of a split in the ranks of the revolutionists on the occasion of discussing the new constitution which had encouraged Louis XVI in his course. Ill-advised by his councilors, he delayed sanctioning the antifeudal decrees and the Declaration of Rights, while secretly giving the order for a detachment of foreign troops in his service to march on Versailles.

When the Parisians, already whipped up over the constitutional debates and bitter about the continuing bread shortage, learned of the king's new provocations, they responded by marching on Versailles to force his hand. La Fayette and the National Guard reluctantly followed the crowd, hours later. La Fayette welcomed the opportunity to remain in reserve, a potential mediator or savior. For a short time Louis XVI contemplated flight rather than yield to the crowd. Finally, he agreed to ratify the decrees, dismiss the troops, and reprovision Paris. A day later, on October 6, under the pressure of an unruly mob which had invaded the royal palace, the king promised that he and his family would move from Versailles and take up residence in Paris. The assembly followed him ten days later. (*See Reading 7, No. I D.*) The Parisian revolutionists held the destiny of the Revolution in their hands.

The Work of the Constituent Assembly, 1789-1791. With their immediate future secure, the deputies tackled the great task before them. Guided by the cahiers, they demolished the old and built the new. Never was so much destroyed in so little time. Yet months elapsed before the old relations were ended and the old personnel replaced by the new, for rapid as the changes were, they were necessarily put into effect piecemeal.

Personal rivalries and ambitions, as well as party differences, pitted individual deputies against each other. There was La Fayette, the would-be George Washington of France, and the champion of the quixotic notion of rallying the king and the nobility to the revolutionary cause. Honest but not strikingly able, he encountered the opposition of the leftist "Triumvirate" of Barnave, Duport, and Charles de Lameth, who mistrusted both the king and the old nobility. He also had a formidable rival in the able, free-wheeling Mirabeau, foe of privilege and radicalism and advocate of a parliamentary system with a strong royal executive and responsible ministers.

Within the assembly, where the revolutionists had divided into a Left, Center, and Right, more or less akin to modern political groups, the Patriots, as the revolutionaries of the Left called themselves, were in control. They also had contacts and supporters outside, in the clubs, the press, the National Guard, and the new municipalities. Of the clubs, the most influential was the network of Jacobin societies which extended over the whole country and linked the regional groups to the Paris Jacobins. The leading deputies were members of the Paris club (officially called the Society of the Friends of the Constitution) in which the cream of the bourgeoisie was enrolled. Little by little the Jacobins became the most powerful of all the pressure groups, functioning virtually like a government party. Newspapers were numerous in and out of Paris and reflected all shades of opinion. Although small in format and inaccurate in their news, they were cheap, widely circulated, and eagerly read. And for several years the press was free.

The National Guard began to form regional federations at which their delegates (*fédérés*) swore an oath of loyalty to each other and to the king, the law, and the nation. On July 14, 1790, the first anniversary of the fall of the Bastille, the gatherings culminated in the stirring *Fête de la Fédération* at Paris. The ceremony took place in the Champ-de-Mars in the presence of the royal family, the deputies, and an immense crowd of spectators. Before these *fédérés* from all over France and delegates from the army and the fleet, Talleyrand celebrated mass and La Fayette administered the oath. (*See Reading 7, No. II A.*)

Moderates and conservatives, those for whom the Revolution was proceeding too rapidly and who distrusted the increasingly democratic temper of the Jacobins, also had their journals and clubs. Well organized, too, were the out-and-out enemies of the Revolution, the "Blacks," who sat on the extreme Right of the assembly and had extensive contacts with counter-revolutionaries in and out of France. At the other end of the political spectrum were the workers. In the beginning, they accepted the leadership of the bourgeois deputies, but soon they, too, had their own popular societies and journals,

their leaders, and a program of action far more democratic than that of the Patriots in the assembly and the
Jacobins outside. So prorevolutionary and antirevolution-
ary forces, covering a wide range of ideas and men, con-
fronted each other, as the deputies of the Constituent
Assembly demolished old France and rebuilt it with more
modern material.

The constitution which the deputies of the Third Estate
had sworn to give France was drafted article by article
and accepted by Louis XVI in September 1791—hence
its name, Constitution of 1791. By its provisions the
enumerated powers of the king were deliberately, even
flagrantly, restricted, while the powers of future assemblies were made very extensive, a transfer of authority
which Louis XVI protested bitterly. Pending the acceptance of this first written constitution in French history,
effective control over policy and legislation remained
firmly in the hands of the Constituent Assembly and its
standing executive committees, which Louis XVI resented
not less heatedly. Their liberalism notwithstanding, the
middle-class deputies strongly doubted the capacity of the
poor and uneducated for self-government. While the
constitution gave French citizens political rights, some
were "active" citizens and others "passive." Tax and
property qualifications disbarred almost half the male
adult population from the exercise of the suffrage. Even
more demanding qualifications restricted the number of
eligible candidates and secondary electors. Of the latter,
in a nation of 25,000,000 people, there were no more
than 50,000 citizens. The slogan might well have been,
"All power to the bourgeoisie."

The cahiers had complained about both the crushing
royal centralization that stifled individual political expression and the separatist privileges of the provinces
which made national unity impossible. The reorganization
of the administrative system met the criticism. It established eighty-three new departments of approximately
equal size in place of the historic provinces. Each department was divided into districts, districts subdivided into
cantons, and cantons into communes. The all-powerful
intendants, with their extraordinary range of authority
and competence for good and evil, gave up their offices,

to be replaced by elected officials. By the terms of the constitution the newly-enfranchised citizens were empowered to elect their own officials at each level of the administrative pyramid, in the eighty-three departments at the summit and the 44,000 communes at the base. These changes went too far in the direction of administrative decentralization, and they were effected too rapidly. They placed upon inexperienced Frenchmen, suddenly faced with civic responsibilities for which they had no training (and frequently no time), burdens which they could not bear. Within two years, the administration of the country was centralized again, under the revolutionaries.

The Constituent Assembly also went a long distance in answering the criticism in the cahiers concerning confusing principles of law and inequitable judicial procedures. It abolished, to begin with, the fantastic medley of courts—royal and administrative, ecclesiastical, feudal, and manorial—which had hampered and delayed justice as much as they had served it. Magistrates who had bought their offices were replaced, like the old intendants, by elected officials. Justice was made free—an incalculable boon—and all citizens, religion and social status notwithstanding, became equal before the law. The highly criticized procedure was greatly simplified and made uniform, like the administrative system, for all France. The bizarre assortment of laws, statutes, and customs, some derived from the principles of Roman law, others from the tribal law of the Germans, was attacked at its root. Time did not permit the deputies to go beyond this herculean destruction and put the new legislation concerning persons and property into a single code. But the idea was repeatedly voiced in the assemblies that there should be a single code of civil laws for the entire kingdom.

There was also a sweeping reformation of the taxation system. The salt tax, execrated by all, as well as the other indirect taxes, was abolished. In accordance with the principle of proportionate equality of taxpayers, the assembly voted three direct taxes payable by all Frenchmen. Since agriculture was the great source of wealth and revenue, the most important of the new taxes was the land tax. This was a triumph for the Physiocrats. There was also a tax on revenue derived from industry and a third tax upon commercial ventures, including a license fee for the exercise of a trade. These reforms were sound enough. With the modifications introduced later in the decade they served France until the First World War. But the data as well as the personnel for their just application were lacking in these years, and the financial stringency of the assembly grew worse.

As the financial situation became desperate, the deputies had no alternative but to take over and nationalize the property of the Church, which they then put up for sale. At the same time the state assumed the debt of the clergy and undertook to pay salaries of the priests and defray the costs of worship, poor relief, and education. With this vast landed property as collateral, the assembly then issued negotiable paper, *assignats,* to cover the sales operation. The assignats soon became a true paper money with the force of legal tender. By the end of 1791 some 2,000,000,000 livres in assignats were in circulation. They were ultimately to collapse in a runaway inflation, but their value to the revolutionary government was enormous. They saved it from bankruptcy, stimulated economic enterprise, and linked thousands and thousands of purchasers of Church lands to the Revolution.

In keeping with their ideals of national unity and free individual enterprise, the deputies removed as much as they could the traditional economic controls and regulations. They ended monopolies and exclusive privileges, suppressed internal customs, abolished the guilds, and restored free trade in grain. By their legislation, however, they also alienated the poor peasants and the city workers. Peasants resented the terms established by the assembly to compensate the former lords of the manor. Not until 1793 did the revolutionary assemblies abolish all manorial rights without any compensation whatsoever to the former landlords. Landless peasants were bitter over the division of the village commons as well as over encroachments upon their collective rights. Under the sales conditions established by the assembly most peasants found it difficult to purchase the nationalized property.

Town workers resented decrees forbidding collective petitions and bargaining, demonstrations and strikes, and

membership in workingmen's unions. They complained
of the inadequate provisions for the destitute and the
absence of public instruction for the ignorant. Most of
the complaining workers were "passive" citizens, dis-
qualified to vote. For them all the Revolution had not
gone far enough. In the young deputy, Maximilien Robespierre, they had a resolute champion of their claims
(*see Reading 7, No. II B, C*); but most of his colleagues
were by 1791 thoroughly frightened by the growing
democratic and radical movement.

The deputies were more frightened still by the violent
counter-revolutionary movement of the Right. Passionate
resentment over the religious policy of the government
united landlords and peasants, ecclesiastics and burghers,
and many workers, too, in a common opposition. The
clergy had been hard hit by the abolition of the tithe and
the loss of the great revenue they had derived from their
confiscated property. Yet the first reform measures, such
as the abolition of monastic vows and the suppression of
many monasteries and convents, were quietly received.
Nor did the restitution of the confiscated estates of the
Huguenots or the grant of full citizenship rights to Jews
and Protestants arouse violent opposition. It was not until
the deputies voted the Civil Constitution of the Clergy in
mid-1790 that grave difficulties arose. Dogma was not
involved in that measure; all that the nationalist reformers intended was to coordinate the administrative
or civil aspects of religious service with the new civil
administration itself. Thus the number of dioceses was
reduced to eighty-three, making one bishopric for each
department; all ecclesiastical offices were to be filled by
election; all priests became salaried officials of the state;
and bishops were forbidden to recognize the administrative authority of the pope.

The decree was duly sanctioned by the king and promulgated by the assembly. To the astonishment and consternation of the deputies nearly all the bishops refused
to take the required oath to support the constitution (of
which the Civil Constitution of the Clergy was technically
a part), and more than 50 per cent of the parish priests
took a similar stand. While millions of parishioners subsequently continued to take the sacraments from the

juring or constitutional clergy, millions also remained
loyal to the nonjuring or refractory clergy. No other
measure harmed the revolutionary cause so much. France
was splitting in two, and Pope Pius VI's formal denunciation of the Civil Constitution completed the schism. The
fires of religious fanaticism were lighted, as from each
side came increasing violence and persecution.

The War and the Overthrow of the Monarchy, 1792.
International politics went on as usual during alterations
in France. Not only did divided, revolutionary France
hold no threat to the European balance, but the powers
were already deeply engaged in armed conflict with one
another. By 1791, however, they began to take alarm.
The same French assembly that had openly disavowed
wars of conquest was threatening the European order
more subtly. In abolishing feudalism and extending application of the decrees to Alsace the deputies infringed
upon the rights of German princes which had been
guaranteed by international treaties. At the request of
the inhabitants the assembly annexed the papal enclave
of Avignon to France, but it did so without the assent of
its sovereign, the pope.

Gradually, the powers saw the wisdom of composing
their differences. Russia concluded peace with Sweden
and Turkey. Austria and Prussia reached an agreement
to safeguard their interests in Poland and also agreed to
make common cause in behalf of the French rulers. Up to
the spring of 1791, however, the Emperor Leopold had
given no heed to the plea of the émigrés that he intervene
with his troops in French affairs. His consistent advice
to his sister, Marie Antoinette, had been that she make
her peace with the revolutionists. In May, 1791, he received a fateful message informing him that the secret
preparations to escape from Paris which the royal couple
had been making for half a year were now completed.
(*See Reading 9, No. 1 A.*) Anxiously, Leopold awaited
developments.

The tragedy of delays, errors, and miscalculations
which reached its dramatic climax in the king's arrest at
Varennes (June 22, 1791), not far from his ultimate
destination on the eastern frontier, had decisive repercus-
sions in the field of international relations. Until it be-

came known that Louis XVI had been stopped and was on his way back to Paris, a prisoner, most deputies feared war, certain that the powers would invade France. After his return, it was the danger of his dethronement and the establishment of a republic that gave cause for alarm. To keep the monarchs from intervening to save their royal colleague, while at the same time rolling back the swelling tide of democratic republicanism (*see Reading 9, No. I C*), the Barnave group put pressure upon the assembly to vote two measures. The first was to absolve Louis XVI from blame for his flight, which was formally designated as an "abduction," and the second, to suspend him from office pending his acceptance of a revised constitution which would be modified to meet the sharp criticism he had made of it on the eve of his flight.

The measures were voted without serious opposition, but the expected tranquillity did not descend upon Paris. The popular clubs and the section assemblies persevered in their agitation for a republic. Both frightened and indignant over this campaign, Barnave and his assembly associates, Bailly, the mayor of Paris, and La Fayette, commanding the National Guard of the city, determined to crush the radical movement. They found their opportunity on July 17, when disorder broke out on the Champ-de-Mars in connection with the signing of a petition which called for the dethronement of Louis XVI. Acting quickly, the authorities proclaimed martial law and summoned the crowd to disperse. An altercation ensued and in the course of it, the National Guard fired upon the petitioners and spectators, killing fifty of them or more.

Within the assembly the relieved representatives of the people congratulated one another on the suppression of subversive radicalism. (*See Reading 9, No. 1 D.*) Outside the assembly a large group of Jacobins temporarily withdrew from the mother society, forming a rival club, called the Feuillants, in protest against passing Jacobin support of one of the antimonarchical petitions. For the moment the moderates had prevailed, but the Paris workers never forgot the "massacre of the Champ-de-Mars"; nor did they ever forgive Barnave, Bailly, or La Fayette.

Leopold himself was canny enough during this critical period to let well enough alone, counting quite sensibly on the revision of the constitution to strengthen the king's position. But he was under heavy pressure to make a gesture in behalf of his sister. Accordingly, in the small town of Pillnitz in Saxony, on August 27, 1791, he and Frederick William of Prussia issued a joint declaration. This famous Declaration of Pillnitz bespoke their desire for an honorable and just settlement of the troubled affairs in France and expressed the hope that the powers would act in concert to that end. (*See Reading 9, No. 1 E.*) "Then and in that case," the statement went on, Austria and Prussia would be ready to act with sufficient troops. Since the likelihood for the visible future was nonexistent that the powers would act in concert, the qualifying phrase was a pure face-saving device for the harassed Leopold. And for the next six months, up to the time of his sudden death, he adhered to his determination not to intervene by force in French affairs. (*See Reading 9, No. 11 A.*) Yet it cannot be denied that the language of Pillnitz, whatever the Emperor's intentions, was provocative, contributing to the growing war temper.

Unfortunately, too, Leopold's son and successor, Francis, and his foreign minister, Kaunitz, were not the only warmongers. They had their counterparts in France. The Feuillants, whom Louis XVI chose to advise him in the new Legislative Assembly, were pacific enough, and the king himself asked no more from Leopold than an armed demonstration at the frontiers. (*See Reading 9, No. 1 B.*) The military adventurer, the Count of Narbonne, however, who had the war office in the Feuillant ministry, was set for war. A successful war, he held, would put the military in control of his country.

In the assembly, too, there were deputies who favored war with Austria. They were then called Brissotins, after the journalist Brissot, who was their great leader; they are better known as Girondins, many of them coming from the department of the Gironde. They were linked with powerful shipping and mercantile interests which favored war for business reasons. Young, romantic, patriotic and idealistic, they believed in full sincerity that war would unmask "traitors" in their midst—meaning the king and the queen—and would be overwhelmingly successful. Besides, they were utterly convinced that "enslaved" Belgians and Rhinelanders would rise up in arms in response to the crusade of the French liberators against "tyrants." (*See Reading 9, No. II D.*)

Narbonne himself fell from office, for his tactics were too hasty, but in the predominantly Girondin ministry which took over, the key office of minister of foreign affairs was held by General Dumouriez. And Dumouriez wanted war for much the same reasons that Narbonne had wanted it: to increase the prestige of the military and use that enhanced power against the Jacobins in behalf of the king. A handful of democrats, Robespierre among them, held out against war; but outside the assembly and within, enthusiasm was overwhelming, and on April 20, the deputies declared war upon Austria.

The war went badly from the very start. (*See Reading 9, No. II C.*) To Brissot's propaganda effort there was no immediate response. Similarly, Dumouriez's diplomatic campaign collapsed; not only did England not cooperate with France, but Prussia entered the lists against her. Fortunately, Frederick William's preoccupation with the coming partition of Poland delayed the active Prussian war effort, a respite of incalculable benefit for the sorely pressed French troops that were staggering under reverses.

Louis XVI for his part had anticipated defeat (*see Reading 9, II B*), expecting his disillusioned subjects to throw themselves into his arms and beg to be saved. On the contrary, a fierce nationalist and revolutionary fury seized the patriots and propelled them to action against both king and the foreign foe. In part this mood reflected class feeling. The assignat was tumbling fast; food prices were soaring and food was hard to get, for peasants were concealing their stocks rather than sell for paper money. Speculators were making a killing by withholding supplies from the market. Heavy government purchases for the troops accentuated the shortages. Again food convoys were attacked and granaries pillaged, and again rioters sacked food shops in the towns and cities. A second revolution, the revolution of the poor, threatened the middle-class deputies who had brought about a disastrous war.

The mood was patriotic and nationalist as well, sustained by hatred for the enemy abroad and the concealed foes at home. The National Guard of Marseilles, trudging the long dusty roads to Paris, lustily chanted the strains of a new song—the *Marseillaise,* it was called—and they knew in their hearts, these "children of the *patrie,*" that they were marching against the "bloody standards of tyranny." The Paris radicals made the fédérés welcome, the fédérés fraternized with the members of the section assemblies, and plans to unmask the "traitors" were drawn up.

The first move of Parisian *sectionnaires* and fédérés from the departments failed on June 20, the anniversary of the Tennis Court Oath, when they invaded the royal palace. Within six weeks they struck again, impelled as before by their fear, not entirely unjustified, of a counter-revolutionary plot. They were terrified also by the Austrian and Prussian troops poised at the French frontier, awaiting the command to advance. At this juncture their almost pathological obsession that the émigrés and monarchs abroad were acting in collusion with secret counter-revolutionaries inside France seemed confirmed by the terms of a statement issued in the name of the Duke of Brunswick, the commanding officer of the allied forces. Drafted for him by one of the émigrés at Coblentz in the Rhineland, the Manifesto declared that the allies were advancing to restore the royal authority; and should any harm be done to the royal family, it continued, Paris would be sacked and burned to the ground.

Instead of intimidating the Parisians, this stupidly phrased manifesto in the war of nerves only enraged the would-be insurrectionists further. With fury in their hearts they struck first, before Brunswick could move. An Insurrectionary Commune took over the municipal administration and directed the successful attack of August 10 when the Paris revolutionists took the royal palace by storm. The king and queen fled for safety to the assembly hall. The republic was not yet officially proclaimed, but it already existed *de facto*. The monarchy had fallen, the most ancient and venerable in Europe. The experiment in a constitutional monarchy had failed.

The arrest of the king, the abrogation of the Constitution of 1791, and the decision to hold elections for a new assembly with constitution-making authority did not end the emergency. Imprisoned the king was indeed, but were not his fellow conspirators still at large, asked the patriots, free to carry out their infamous assignments? So under the instructions of the new municipal government patrols of troops arrested suspects on the streets, while house-to-house search parties dislodged other "enemies." Arrests, however, were not enough; how could volunteers, responding to Danton's stirring appeal, leave for the war front while prisons were gorged with fifth-columnists whom a prison-break—such as had taken place elsewhere —could easily release? Obviously, elementary precaution commanded that they be tried—and of course condemned. Thus began the "trials" of the prisoners on September 2, and for four days they continued until about 1,200 victims had been put to death. Only a minority of these unfortunates were political suspects or refractory priests; most of them were common law prisoners.

The public authorities were helpless before the panic fear and the homicidal fury that gripped the killers. Whether public opinion approved or condemned at that time is difficult to say; but there was no open condemnation of the butchery of the "September massacres" until after the great fear had subsided. For several weeks more the Prussians threatened, but on September 20, the very day that the newly elected deputies of the National Convention met for the first time, the republican troops turned Brunswick's men back at Valmy in the Argonne passes.

Revolution and the Western World, 1789-1792. News of the upheaval in France spread to the outside world, crossing the mountains and the rivers of the European continent, leaping across the Channel, spanning the broad Atlantic. From Paris political refugees and sympathetic travelers, returning to their homes, disseminated the good tidings to the neighboring states. Newspapers with accounts of the legislative debates and the text of the decrees, cheap pamphlets, private letters, and word-of-mouth reports conveyed to a wide audience the details of the astounding storm that had blown up in France.

Not to all Europe, however. Distance and intellectual backwardness kept the news out of northern, southern, and eastern Europe, as did royal absolutism and aristocratic control. Only in Poland were the reformers strong enough to act upon their enthusiasm. Elsewhere, in Russia, Scandinavia, Hungary, in southern Italy, Spain and Portugal, the established order held fast, undisturbed by revolutionary threats, even by exact information. In these states the population was predominantly rural, and by themselves peasants were powerless. Tradition, inertia, the habit of obedience prevailed.

On the other hand, since their contacts with France were close and of long standing, the peoples inhabiting the tier of states along the eastern frontier responded at once to the news of what was happening in France. Whether in the distorted version which émigrés gave to it or in the embellished form of French sympathizers, in the towns and the countryside from Holland to northern Italy, the news was heatedly received and vigorously discussed. The reception of the news was all the more heated in the Austrian Netherlands because these regions had known revolutionary strife before 1789. Not until later in the decade, however, did revolution break out again in this area, and along the left bank of the Rhine, in Switzerland and in northern Italy, too, not until the French troops arrived to give native revolutionists the necessary help. Meantime, ferment was high.

The Germanies.   Further to the east in the disunited Germanies within the Holy Roman Empire, the French Revolution made slight impact. Here and there local peasant uprisings disturbed the bucolic peace, but never did rural unrest seriously endanger the feudal regime. In small towns and cities, too, life pursued its even course, following familiar grooves. To the orderly, law-abiding German burghers the aggrieved workers looked in vain for guides to lead them into revolutionary action. German intellectuals, on the other hand, men of letters, artists, professors and students, exulted over the first news from Paris. The venerable Kant and the young Fichte, the cosmopolitan savant from Mainz, Georg Forster, the aging Wieland and the youthful Gentz, all rang the changes until they were disillusioned, on the triumph of reason, freedom, the goodness of man, and the liberation of mankind from its fetters. (*See Reading 8, No. I A-C.*) But they and all the other representatives of the *Aufklärung*—not excluding Goethe and Schiller who in their

views on revolution advanced from mistrust to aversion—
made hardly any impression on circles outside their own
little private worlds. They had no tug from reality. It was
as though they wrote and spoke for one another. To
German life they imparted no new impulse.

Great Britain. Life did not remain in its familiar
grooves in Great Britain. The United Kingdom was not
the disunited Germanies. Englishmen had already made
their revolution and had long experience in self-government. The principles of popular sovereignty and the right
of resistance to oppression, however blurred in practice,
were still honored as rights natural to freeborn Englishmen. There was in 1789 considerable prosperity and complete security for the government; there was also in England and Scotland and Wales a deeply-rooted discontent
against the plutocracy of shipping magnates, financiers,
entrepreneurs, and landed aristocrats who, supported by
and supporting the established Church, were solidly en-
trenched in power. And in these early years of revolution,
from 1789 to 1792, the disaffected found an opportunity
by approving developments in France to give voice to
their criticism of policies of the government at home.

An immediate response to the news from France came
from the youth. It came also from humanitarian poets and
from dissenting clergymen. "It's coming yet for a' that,"
rejoiced Robert Burns, "that man to man the world o'er,
shall brothers be for a' that." The celebrated Unitarian
clergyman, Dr. Price, gave thanks to the Lord in a highly
publicized sermon for permitting him to live long enough
to see "thirty million peoples demanding liberty with
an irresistible voice." In posters, broadsides, pamphlets,
and periodical press, Englishmen hailed the destruction
of the Bastille and the abolition of the feudal regime.
From the pulpits of Non-Conformists and in the House
of Commons, on tavern floors and the stages of theaters,
on the streets, in schoolrooms and salons, enthusiasts lifted
up their hearts over the glad tidings.

Edmund Burke soon sounded the conservative alarm
gun, loudly and effectively. His *Reflections on the Revolution in France*, which was published in the autumn of
1790, was a masterly indictment of revolutionary principles. It was also the classical defense of conservatism

against eighteenth-century liberalism. Denying the valid-
ity of natural rights and stressing the claims of history,
of past tradition and present interest, Burke poured out
his wrath on the revolutionists in France who were jump-
ing Niagara. (*See Reading 8, No. II A.*) Scores of writers
rushed into the literary arena to refute him, and none
was so eloquent or so convincing as that pamphleteer of
genius Tom Paine. In a few months he composed his
Rights of Man (spring of 1791) which passionately defended natural rights and the sovereignty of the people.
No other book was so widely read or so influential in
the democratic cause as that emphatic affirmation of the
right of the people, not merely once when they made their
constitution, but at all times to order their destiny according to the general will. (*See Reading 8, No. II B.*)

In this setting of intense public controversy, the advocates of political reform made great strides forward.
The semimoribund Revolution Society of 1688 resumed
its meetings. Under the leadership of honest Horne Tooke,
old-fashioned liberals revived the lagging Society for
Constitutional Information. In Parliament, reformers like
Fox and Grey broke with Pitt and founded in the spring
of 1792 the Society of the Friends of the People toward
which gravitated men of easy circumstances and moderate
views. The most spectacularly effective, however, of the
political clubs was the London Corresponding Society
which the Scottish-born cobbler, Thomas Hardy, imbued
with his own ardent democratic faith. Weavers, mechanics,
carpenters, cabinet workers, artisans of all crafts, enrolled
by the thousands in this "poor man's reform club." Dues
were only a penny a week, local chapters met frequently,
once a week, and delegates went back and forth between
the London club and its affiliates in the industrial towns
of Sheffield, Manchester, and Birmingham, as well as
from centers in distant Scotland.

The democratic tide reached crest in the late summer
of 1792. Then it ran out, for with the news of the downfall of the French monarchy, the September massacres,
and the advance of the French republican troops into
Belgium, the governing classes of England were swept
by fear. All hope of parliamentary reform vanished.
Ministers and journalists fulminated against the atheists

across the Channel. Patriotic mobs attacked the dangerous admirers of the French. The homes of sympathizers were sacked. Paine was tried for seditious libel, fortunately for himself, *in absentia,* while the law courts prosecuted printers and booksellers. Pitt, slowly preparing his country for war in defense of England's national interests, denounced the political societies as unpatriotic, and his government did not disdain the use of secret informers and manufactured evidence to maintain British law and order.

The reaction was in full swing when England went to war in February 1793, and in Ireland too. The democratic strivings of the Irish malcontents had been encouraged by the successful American Revolution. Their religious grievances against the Anglican Church and their burning hopes of national independence brought together into a single group Protestants and Catholics. Though the frightened authorities were taking legal action against their Society of United Irishmen by the end of 1792, they could not break the cadres of the movement. Insurrection in Ireland was not far distant.

The United States. The rage for liberty was widespread in the United States. Indeed, nowhere else in the world was the democratic creed so broadly diffused, so tenaciously held. Thanks in large measure to their own historical experience, millions of Americans had learned unquestioningly to accept what Tom Paine expounded so magnificently for them, the autonomy and dignity of human personality, the rule of law and popular sovereignty, the equality of rights for all.

To defend and maintain those rights they had fought a revolutionary struggle which ended in victory. Yet when the first news of the hurricane in France reached American shores, it fell upon a tense and troubled political scene. The rugged individualists who had waged the revolutionary struggle against England felt that they had been cheated of the fruits of victory by their own compatriots. Farmers and frontiersmen, mechanics, artisans and small merchants, soldiers and sailors, and many members of the liberal professions burned with resentment against the wealthy and prosperous who in the years following the Revolutionary War had dammed up the

Spirit of 1776. Feelings were running high in 1789 against the great New England merchants, Virginia aristocrats, and landowners of New York state. The situation was troubled, almost explosive, as the newly inaugurated hero-president, George Washington, moved with his government to the seat of Federalist strength in Philadelphia. Leaders and followers, as they began their great debates on the pressing issues confronting the new nation, argued and discussed in an atmosphere complicated still further by the exhilarating or disturbing news from Europe.

At first there was almost universal enthusiasm. (*See Reading 8, No. III A*.) Such a response was not unnatural, for America and France were linked by many ties. Americans were in gratitude bound to France for the aid that it had given them by the alliance of 1778. Many Americans, Jefferson among them, were convinced and pleased that it was the example of the thirteen colonies which had fired the spark of revolution in France. (*See Reading 8, No. III B*.) As the Revolution grew more radical, American conservatives went openly into the opposition and liberals lapsed into disillusioned silence. All that the Federalists stood for—peace and prosperity, trade and good relations with England, a strong central government—was menaced by a movement that challenged authority and fixed principles, and proclaimed the sovereignty of the people. (*See Reading 8, No. III C.*) With equal fervor the anti-Federalists, soon to call themselves Republicans, who stood for a broader democracy of small independent farmers and a looser form of government, were convinced that the future of the America that they loved was inextricably linked with the success of the French Revolution.

Debate on the issues at home blended with the defense or the condemnation of the revolution abroad. The business interests and the moneyed men rallied around Alexander Hamilton and the solution which he advocated for the future of his country: the assumption of the debt of the states and the funding of the national debt; the establishment of the Bank of the United States; the excise tax on whisky; protective tariffs and good trade relations with England. But all these measures were staunchly disputed by Jefferson and his supporters, who held that under the sharp debates in Congress on all those measures, the real issue at stake was democracy itself, the issue of whom the new legislation would benefit, the issue of who was to rule at home in the country that had won home rule.

This great continuing debate by the Founding Fathers was relatively free from violence in the years from 1789 to 1792, even though the columns of the highly partisan press were heated enough. The pro-Federalist newspapers, quite understandably, were more numerous than those of their opponents, and in them the two Adamses, John and John Quincy, found space for the expression of their conservative anti-French views. Perhaps of all the Federalist spokesmen the most persuasive was John Fenno, editor of the *Gazette of the United States,* whom Hamilton supported in more than one way. Benjamin Franklin's grandson, "Benny" Bache hit back at Fenno with biting words in the columns of the *Aurora* which he edited. But most of all, it was on the caustic pen of the poet of two revolutions, Philip Freneau, that the democrats counted. Editor during all of its brief existence of the *National Gazette* which Jefferson helped to support, he was the journalistic bugbear and the terror of all the Federalists.

The calm was broken in the closing months of 1792 when word came that France had overthrown the monarchy and had proclaimed the Republic, and that the embattled French troops were hurling back the armies of the German "tyrants." But it was not until France went to war with England that the floodgates of happiness were opened and Americans went wild with enthusiasm in the mad year of 1793.

THE NATIONAL CONVENTION, 1792-1795

Establishing the "Revolutionary Government." The National Convention was no more united than the preceding assemblies. Once the new deputies had formally declared the monarchy abolished and decreed that henceforth all public documents should be dated "Year I of the French Republic," agreement ended. A fierce, murderous struggle for political control then broke out between the Girondin deputies of the Right and the Montagnards on the Left. The Montagnards (literally the mountaineers, from the high tier of seats on which they sat) were the deputies who supported the policies of the Paris delegation, all of whom were members of the Jacobins. Although the Girondins were also once members of the Society, most of them had now been expelled.

Personal rivalries entered into the fray. Leading Girondins, such as Brissot, Condorcet, Vergniaud, Roland, feared and were jealous of Montagnard leaders, particularly of Danton. Brissot and Robespierre, who had clashed over foreign policy, were the bitterest of enemies. The morbidly suspicious Marat was hated by all the Girondins. Sharp disagreement over the role that Paris should play in the revolutionary movement also set the groups apart, but most of all they were divided by their divergent social views and conception of political tactics. Where the Girondins opposed governmental regulation of economic activities, the Montagnards, who were not less middle class in social origins and certainly as property-minded, realistically accepted the necessity of instituting controls at least for the duration. To avoid being swamped by the militant masses who had already overwhelmed the preceding national assembly, they were prepared to pursue a loose welfare-state policy favoring the "have-nots" against the "haves."

Before long the Girondins dissipated much of their original superiority of numbers and support. The militant Paris democrats were openly charging that they were no longer true to their revolutionary faith. By their tactics first in obstructing the trial of Louis XVI for intelligence with the enemy and then in endeavoring to save him after he had been found guilty by the Convention, the Girondins only deepened those suspicions. The trial of the king had begun early in December; by mid-January 1793, the deputies returned a verdict of guilty and condemned him by a bare plurality of one vote to immediate execution. The unfortunate monarch was guillotined on January 21, 1793, a victim of his weaknesses, bad faith, and almost incredible political obtuseness. An official proclamation announced to France that all true patriots approved of his punishment; in reality, bewilderment and fear gripped many hearts. (*See Reading 10, No. II, A and B.*)

Until the trial the Girondins still enjoyed the prestige that sprang from military victory. While the Prussian forces slowly withdrew from French soil after Valmy, the French republican troops were moving steadily into enemy territory, and on November 6, at Jemappes in Belgium, General Dumouriez won a smashing victory over the Austrians which opened the Netherlands to his advancing armies. At the same time other French forces overran the left bank of the Rhine. The jubilant Girondin deputies called again for a crusade of "peoples" against "kings," and on November 19, 1792, the assembly voted a propaganda decree which extended French fraternity and offered French assistance to all people who wished to recover their liberty. (*See Reading 10, No. I A.*)

Propaganda warfare was complemented by more old-fashioned commercial warfare. The Convention proclaimed that the Scheldt River was now open to the shipping of all states, thus striking a heavy blow to the trade of Holland and its English protector. Territorial expansion accompanied commercial warfare. Savoy, Nice, and Belgium were annexed by the Convention; part of the left bank of the Rhine also, and the rest occupied by French troops. On December 15 came the second propaganda decree putting French conquest on a pay-as-you-go basis, payment to come from the liberated peoples in return for the advantages of having French soldiers set up revolutionary rule in their lands. (*See Reading 10, No. I B.*)

The liberated peoples could only protest and fume, but the British government swung into action. The swift developments of the last several months had at last convinced Pitt that the national interests of England were in danger. Accordingly, he prepared his countrymen for the coming of war. (*See Reading 11, No. I A.*) By February 1, 1793, France and Great Britain were at war and within several months Pitt became the paymaster of the First Coalition. France was at war with most of Europe.

The Girondins were the first to suffer from the extension of the war. In the Vendée, in western France, peasants rebelled openly against the assembly. Incited by secret royalist agents and local nonjuring priests, the Vendeans rose up in arms against the levy of soldiers for the fighting front. In Paris and other large cities food prices, bread in particular, which had been stabilized during the past year, began rising sharply again. Fats, sugar, and coffee, also soaps, were not to be had. Once more speechmakers whipped up the sectionnaires and again the hungry masses pillaged foodshops. The working classes had new leaders now, Enragés (or mavericks) they were called, who pressed urgent demands on the deputies for the introduction of price controls, legislation against hoarders, decrees to ensure rationing and requisitioning of supplies, and more rigorous security measures against internal enemies.

At this juncture General Dumouriez deserted the republican cause. Long a bitter if secret enemy of the Jacobins, he had been outraged by the guillotining of the king and had vehemently protested against the propaganda decrees and the annexation policy. Upon the Jacobin leaders he placed responsibility for the loss of the Belgium that he had conquered in the preceding fall. He ordered his troops to march on Paris, but they refused to follow him, so he crossed the Austrian line seeking safety. Paris itself was safe, but because of his defection the French troops along the middle Rhine were forced to fall back before the Prussians, while the northeast fighting front was glaringly exposed.

The deputies improvised emergency measures to save the *patrie*. They sent out representatives-on-mission with discretionary authority to the rebellious departments. They set up local surveillance committees and military commissions which were empowered to execute within twenty-four hours all rebels caught under arms. Within the assembly an executive committee of elected deputies with strictly limited powers was also established to guide the Convention in formulating policy and coordinating the war effort. In this first Committee of Public Safety, Danton, the presumed hero of August 10, was the leading figure. This first Committee of Public Safety proved ineffective, first because of its restricted powers and even more because of Danton's misguided attempt to conciliate the enemy both within and outside France.

The Girondins, sensing that time was running out, made frantic efforts in the spring of 1793 to keep their control over the assembly. They redoubled their attacks on the outstanding Jacobin leaders. They threatened Paris with destruction, and they incited against the capital the great provincial cities of Bordeaux, Marseilles, Lyons, and Caen. The first counter-attack of the Paris municipality failed on May 31, when the assembly refused to order the arrest of the Girondin leaders. But on June 2, under the orders of the new Insurrectionary Commune which had meantime seized power, the National Guard surrounded the assembly hall and forced the Convention to order the house arrest of the leading Girondin deputies and several of their ministers. Thus Girondin parliamentary obstruction came to an end and without bloodshed. In terms of liberty the revolution of June 2 exacted a heavy price. Parliamentary immunity had been flagrantly violated. Coercion was in the ascendancy, for the shadow of the Insurrectionary Commune fell heavily over the nominal representatives of the people.

Soon the arrested Girondin leaders fled Paris and organized a revolt which spread with amazing rapidity over sixty departments south and west of Paris. In the eyes of the Montagnards, who had proclaimed the Republic "one and indivisible," this Girondin revolt was a "federalist" insurrection, a counter-revolutionary attempt to substitute for the central authority of the Convention, supported by democratic Parisians, a loose federal government resting upon the well-to-do followers of the Girondins in the great provincial cities. Counter-revolutionary it was not originally, but as the revolt spread, it sucked in all shades of counter-revolutionary opposition. The outlook for the Republic was bleak in other parts of France. In the northwest, royalists and Catholics were waging a guerilla warfare without mercy; the Austrians and Prussians, who had followed up their victories of the spring, were now well inside French territory and again the road to Paris was open; on the Mediterranean the great port of Toulon had fallen to the British; in the southeast the Sardinian troops threatened newly-annexed Savoy.

To discredit the propaganda of the rebellious Girondins the Convention hastily drew up and adopted a democratic constitution whose provisions were designed to give the lie to the charges of Jacobin political coercion. At the same time the sorely pressed deputies bid for peasant support by abolishing all the remaining manorial dues without any compensation at all. Meantime the troops on the fighting front fought hard to contain the advancing foe and the Danton Committee continued its negotiations with the enemy for a compromise peace. Not for long in this critical summer of 1793, for the deputies of the assembly rejected the policy of the Committee. Grasping the elemental fact that at this point a negotiated peace could benefit only the victorious Coalition, the deputies voted the Danton Committee out of power on July 10, and in the new Committee of Public Safety the outstanding Jacobin supporters of an aggressive war policy gained control.

The immediate beginnings of the new Committee were not auspicious. The Coalition armies still advanced; the rebels in the Vendée were gaining ground; the stop-gap decrees against hoarding and profiteering proved futile; Marat, the great idol of the Paris populace, was assassinated; the Paris Commune and the sections threatened another *journée*. Slowly, the Grand Committee, as it was later to be called, proved its mettle. After a few weeks the assembly elected Robespierre, the hard-working and austere "Incorruptible" to membership. Shortly thereafter, two distinguished and determined military engineers, Prieur de la Côte d'Or and Lazare Carnot, were also elected, both of whom showed themselves administrators of extraordinary talent. Under their sponsorship in August the Convention voted the epochal and electrifying decree of the levy-in-mass which placed all resources of France, human and material, on call. With the passage of this decree a giant step forward was taken toward total war. (*See Reading 10, No. III B.*)

Early in September, to placate the sections which still threatened insurrectionary action, the Convention elected two of the most unbridled Paris critics to the Committee. Responsibility quickly sobered the newest members. They were twelve now in the seats of power, the men who began to govern France under the slogan that "terror was the order of the day." In mid-September the Committee drafted a draconic Law of Suspects which the Convention voted. (*See Reading 10, No. III C.*) By the end of the month the assembly voted the sweeping Law of the Maximum which made provision for nationwide controls over prices and wages. The Constitution of 1793 had been overwhelmingly ratified by the country. Nevertheless, its application was suspended, and a decree early in October proclaimed that "the government of France was revolutionary until the peace." In short, the legal dictatorship of the Committee of Public Safety had begun. For several months more a succession of *ad hoc* emergency decrees steadily extended the power of this "revolutionary government." In December a comprehensive decree, appropriately called the "Constitution of the Terror" consolidated the preceding legislation into a coordinated whole. This government of the Terror, relentlessly and systematically practicing what Robespierre called a "Despotism of Liberty," was in control of France.

The "Despotism of Liberty." Policy decisions on the highest level were formulated by the Committee of

Public Safety whose members were elected for a month
at a time. In form, all laws, decrees, and regulations were
drawn up in the name of the Convention; in reality, the
theory of the Committee's responsibility to the Convention was something of a fiction. While there were recur-
rent flareups of parliamentary opposition, by and large
for the better part of a year, the deputies rubber-stamped
the Committee's decrees and enacted its proposals into
law. Not that the Committee was as united in its outlook as Prieur de la Côte d'Or later recalled when he
described its work habits and its great achievements. (*See
Reading 10, No. III A.*) But by its brutal energy and its
forcefulness it proved successful, and its success and its
power to coerce and to punish readily induced the deputies to follow its leadership.

In its formative months the central executive government, which also included the Committee of General
Security, had considerable difficulty in imposing its policy
direction both on its liaison agents and the local units of
government. By the end of 1793 many of the virtually
independent deputies-on-mission had been replaced by
the more docile "national agents"; in the towns and
villages the "Popular Societies" and the local revolutionary committees were also well under control, getting
their impetus and initiative from Paris.

This combination of dynamic leadership at the top
and unprecedented release of mass human energy at the
base saved the *patrie*. There was much bungling on the
part of petty officials. There was wide abuse of power by
arbitrary or ambitious administrators. There was grum-
bling, noncooperation, and obstruction from men who
feared or hated the revolutionary government for the
sacrifices it demanded from them. There was divided
counsel in the Committee itself, where the more social-
minded triumvirate of Robespierre, Saint-Just, and Couthon, was at odds with the conservative specialists and
technicians such as Carnot and Prieur. Still the regime of
Terror imposed its will upon the country.

On the local level patriotic vigilantes, whether members of the Jacobin Club or of the more radical clubs,
badgered their fellow-citizens into patriotic conformity.
The local committees issued identity cards (*certificats*

de civisme) and compiled the dread list of suspects. The petty revolutionary courts and military commissions sat in judgment on the accused, giving their verdicts more or less independently of the Revolutionary Tribunal in Paris. Bread was rationed, and in the larger towns where food cards were introduced, the citizens queued up for supplies. Where local needs demanded it, the authorities were empowered to requisition supplies. In all cases food supplies and war materiel were requisitioned for the military at officially fixed prices. While these controls were not always enforced and the black market flourished (*see Reading 10, No. III D*), the economic Terror kept the assignat relatively stable and saved the small consumer from hoarders, speculators, and monopolists. It helped win the war.

Along with the restriction upon political freedom and economic enterprise there were also religious controls. Juring clergy as well as refractory clergy were now engulfed by the mounting tide of revolutionary patriotism. On September 22, 1792, the day following the abolition of the monarchy (by coincidence the day of the autumnal equinox) the deputies had decreed the beginning of a new era and a new year, Year I of the Republic. In the fall of 1793, a revolutionary calendar supplanted the old Christian calendar. According to the new computation of 1793 the year was divided into twelve months of thirty days each, the months to bear such poetic names as Nivôse (month of winter) and Ventôse (month of wind). In this way the Convention sought to substitute "the truths of nature and the realities of reason for priestly prestige and the visions of ignorance." Each month, moreover, so as to do away with the Christian sabbath, was divided into ten-day periods called *décades*. To eliminate the saints' days the ordinary days of the year were to be named for the "true treasures of rural life"—an obvious bid for the support of the recalcitrant peasants who stubbornly kept their Catholic faith.

Thus organized, the Terror government entered upon those activities which gave the name "Great" to the Committee of Public Safety of Year II. With all national resources at its disposal revolutionary France raised, fed, clothed, and equipped fighting forces close to 1,000,000 men. Commanded by new officers, many of them risen from the ranks, sustained by their patriotic fervor, employing the reckless tactics of mass attacks, these troops whose numbers were without precedent in the history of European wars, broke the military threat to revolutionary France. The Federalist revolt was crushed, Toulon recaptured from the English, the Austrian and Prussian armies rolled back to the frontier.

The military threat was dissipated, but the counter-revolutionary enemies remained at home—secret royalist sympathizers, Catholics, Girondin supporters, the "Aristos," and disillusioned bourgeois. Had these true enemies along with many innocent suspects been left to the tender mercies of local stalwarts or the undisciplined personnel of the "revolutionary armies of the interior," their fate could readily have been that of the wretched victims of the September massacres. It was partly to prevent the repetition of September but more to hold the Paris sans-culottes in line by a dramatic demonstration of government power that the two central committees held great state political trials in October and November 1793. On this occasion the knife of the guillotine fell impartially upon such "counter-revolutionaries" as Marie Antoinette, the Duke of Orleans, Barnave, and the leading Girondin leaders of the revolt. All told, in Year II (1793-1794) with some semblance of a formal trial the Terror took the toll of 40,000 men and women. In addition to the people guillotined, suspects crowded the prisons, some 300,000 of them, or even more, nearly all of whom were subsequently released.

The Terror was sweeping in its geographical range. Excepting those instances where the Committee could not control cruel or irresponsible representatives-on-mission, the Terror was not however blind, nor an instrument of class warfare. It was an instrument designed to strike down real and presumed counter-revolutionaries, and statistical study makes clear that its incidence was heaviest where the danger appeared most grave. Into this organized killing and arresting there entered power drives and blood lust as well as obsessive fears for the security of the *patrie*. Embedded too in its homicidal impulses was the utopian ideal of the entire eighteenth century, the dream of eradicating evil and making the world better for man.

At all times the Committee of Public Safety had to cope with political opposition from authentic revolutionaries. The Hébertists were to its Left, rabble-rousing followers of the demagogue Hébert, advocates of strong-arm tactics at home and war to the bitter end abroad. The moderates were to its Right, deputies and nondeputies who rallied around Danton, wishing to relax economic controls, end the political terror, and negotiate peace with the enemy. If Danton, while neither conventionally respectable nor honest to excess, was personally courageous, generous-hearted and a true revolutionary patriot, many of his followers were food speculators, fraudulent war contractors, or otherwise engaged in dubious financial ventures. Hébert was personally irresponsible, and in addition to good patriots who followed him out of conviction, there was also a sprinkling of political opportunists, shady adventurers, and secret foreign agents. In the circumstances it was not difficult for the austere Robespierrists to convince themselves that both sets of opponents were enemies of the *patrie,* members of the vast Foreign Conspiracy which Pitt had organized and financed to crush the Revolution.

The Dantonists, clever tacticians, first joined with the Robespierre group to break the power of the Hébertists. Robespierre, too, played the political game astutely. He had no intention of accepting Dantonist assistance in destroying the exaggerated anti-Christian crusade of the Hébertists in order to further Danton's own campaign for clemency within France and peace with the enemy outside. In two remarkable speeches which give a revealing insight into his political and social philosophy he outlined the goal to which he would bring the Revolution. (*See Reading 10, No. IV A.*) Aware that the Dantonist appeal had struck a deep responsive chord, he served notice in these speeches that the Dantonists too were enemies of his conception of the Revolution. The duel for control of the government ended in the early spring of 1794, when the Robespierrists, supported by the Center of the assembly, crushed first the extremists who supported Hébert and then the moderates who followed Danton.

After parodies of legal trials, both Hébert and Danton were guillotined, their chief subordinates with them.

The crushing of the political opposition coincided in point of time with the military defeat of the foreign foe. On all fronts in this spring of 1794 France was victorious, and the need for the Terror as an instrument of patriotic security seemed to have ended. There was a softening of the economic Terror. Controls over prices were loosened, a development largely benefitting peasant producers whose continued support the Committee required. But this mild relaxation of food prices still further alienated the already hostile city workers who were both bewildered and embittered by the execution of the Enragés and the Hébertist leaders. The political Terror was not relaxed. On the contrary, Robespierre and his two close associates, Saint-Just and Couthon, imposed upon their colleagues in the Committee their own decision to maintain, even extend it.

They were imbued with a messianic sense of mission to usher in the ideal republic. They would pull down to earth the democratic heaven, where each citizen would serve only the general will, where there would be neither rich nor poor, where fraternity would support liberty and equality. At the core of their fanatical zeal to legislate mankind into felicity with the aid of the guillotine was the fervent humanitarian idealism so characteristic of Robespierre himself. But in its coercive mentality and procedure it was the classical Platonic dream of guardians for *hoi-polloi*. It was the despotism of virtue unrestrained by a questioning conscience.

The Robespierrists themselves created the situation out of which their ultimate downfall—at least in retrospect— appeared inescapable. In accordance with their long-range social and economic policy they had the Convention pass the Ventôse decrees which, if carried out, would have established a true peasant democracy. Instead, they only estranged their more property-minded associates of the Committee. By their short-term economic policy, they also antagonized the Parisian workers whose support they lacked when they needed it most. While their religious policy culminated theatrically in the public celebration of a new civic religion, paradoxically this cult of the Supreme Being, which was designed to replace Christianity with a new deistic revolutionary religion, aroused fears that Robespierre was cunningly preparing to restore Catholicism. Meantime, he outraged the detractors whom he already had in the Committee of General Security and terrified his former supporters of the Center in the Convention by a police measure which seemingly stripped them of parliamentary immunity. By this new law the administration of revolutionary justice was completely concentrated in Paris and the range of activities punishable by death was grimly increased.

In the six-week interval which lay between the promulgation of this law and Robespierre's overthrow, the Terror reached its height. Compulsory loyalty to the government had thinned down to an almost transparent veneer over naked resentment, fear, and rage. Most of France hated Robespierre and the Committee which he dominated, awaiting only the right moment to hit out against the Jacobin-terrorist idealists. A small number of deputies-on-mission whom the Committee had recalled to Paris for flagrantly terrorist abuse of authority, organized the attack in the Convention. Knowing that their lives would be forfeit if Robespierre remained in power, they whipped up the fears of the deputies, particularly of the cowed and frightened Center. The Robespierrists, thrown off balance, defended themselves lamely and ineptly on the 9th Thermidor (July 27, 1794) and meekly allowed themselves to be placed under arrest. Late that night when hope of rescue by the Commune failed, Robespierre tried to commit suicide, but he survived his wounds long enough to be guillotined on the following day. The homicidal republic of virtue was now ended, and a torrent of vituperation began to pour over the memory of the "Incorruptible." (*See Reading 10, No. V A.*)

The Thermidorian Reaction, 1794-1795. Thermidor became the great divide of the Revolution. It was a major upheaval, hurling into the discard of history the men, the controls, and the outlooks of the Terror government. The representatives-on-mission who had led the terrified deputies of the Center in overthrowing Robespierre had no intention of relaxing the Terror, even less of ending the dictatorship of the Mountain. Only a few days elapsed before they realized that the 9th of Thermidor was not going to be just another revolutionary *journée,* that the hopes and expectations which Thermidor released were not to be satisfied by substituting one group of revolutionary extremists for another in the seats of power. Denouncing the Robespierrist tyranny had opened the floodgates for the most unrestrained attacks upon the entire regime.

There was a release from the almost unbearable tension and from the restraints of the puritanical Jacobins. In salons, in the columns of the liberated press, on the stage, in gambling halls and on dance floors, exultant French men and women vented their happiness over liberation. The prisons poured forth thousands of suspects. The Girondin deputies who had signed a protest against the arrest of their leaders were readmitted to the sessions of the assembly; even the surviving outlawed leaders of the Federalist revolt were reinstated. So closely was democracy associated in the minds of men with Jacobin violence, that there was much initial approval of the young hoodlums, derisively called "The Gilded Youth," many of them slackers or deserters, who deliberately picked quarrels with well-known Jacobin sympathizers, and approval too of royalists, when they organized noisy demonstrations against the Republic. (*See Reading 10, No. V B.*)

Politically, the fifteen months from July 1794 to the end of October 1795, the Thermidorian Reaction, as the period is known, was a transition from the premature and repudiated experiment in republican democracy to the restored rule of the propertied middle class. The Revolution returned to its course of 1789. One by one, the key institutions of the "revolutionary government" were destroyed. The Thermidorians rescinded the dictatorial powers of the Committee of Public Safety, abolished the local revolutionary committees, repealed the hated police law and finally closed the doors of the Jacobin Club in Paris. Within the Convention itself the moderates got control, and the assembly began to assert in fact as well as in theory its control over the central government and its supervisory authority over the local administration. Thermidorian France was treading the long road which led to true constitutional government.

The victors of Thermidor also attempted to restore normal religious relations, but the moment had not yet come for lasting peace. Despite the almost abject concessions that the Convention made to the refractory clergy, the measures proved insufficient and the fierce religious fighting in the west was only briefly halted. (*See Reading 10, No. V C.*) Moreover, many of the reopened churches which the government placed at the disposal of the nonjuring clergy became centers of joint religious and political opposition. The concurrent effort to win back the support of the constitutional clergy was as little successful as the negotiations with the refractory. The government adopted a new policy of separation, expecting doubtless that disestablishing the Church and depriving ecclesiastics of financial support would starve Catholicism and uproot "the religious superstition," but the intentions of the framers of the law were not realized. (*See Reading 12, No. III.*)

On the other hand, the dismantling of the machinery of the economic Terror was effective. Unfortunately, decontrol led straight to disaster. The Ventôse decrees, which had been designed to transfer the landed property of convicted suspects to the indigent peasantry, were repealed. Against the workings of price controls there had been many complaints, and just ones, but with the repeal of the Law of the Maximum and the end of controls, prices shot up to astronomic heights. The assignat, left unsupported, collapsed completely in value, and the inflation which the Montagnards had painfully held in check now reached the final runaway stage. A bad harvest, continued government requisitions, and virtually unchecked profiteering aggravated the hardships of the poor. Even by revolutionary norms their suffering surpassed all previous heights.

The victims of this catastrophe assailed a government which neither could nor would give adequate relief, and many of them began to regret the good old days of 1793-1794. There were demonstrations against the government in the spring of 1795. But without arms the unhappy Paris sectionnaires were powerless and an uprising of despair was easily crushed by governmental troops. The public authorities and private individuals now took full vengeance against the old terrorists. In the place of the odious Jacobin Terror of 1793-1794, a fierce "White Terror" raged in southern and southwestern France in 1795-1796. The royalist movement was gathering its strength, and the danger was real that either constitutionally, at the forthcoming political elections, or by insurrectionary action, the royalist pretender, the Count of Provence, would grasp power from the faltering republicans.

The military victories of the Republic saved it. A combined English-royalist naval expedition was routed. On land the republican troops continued their triumphant advance of 1794 and swept all before them in the spring campaign of 1795. The Austrian Netherlands were conquered completely for a second time. The natural frontiers were reached again on the middle Rhine. All of Holland was overrun in a brilliant offensive. Most of the generals were in favor of continuing the war, but the civilian directors of policy wished for peace to consolidate the gains of the victorious Republic.

The hard-pressed members of the Coalition were also ready for peace. Prussia was the first to withdraw. By the open terms of the treaty signed at Basel in April 1795, the French forces moved out of Prussian territory on the right bank of the Rhine, but retained possession of the territory conquered on the left bank between the Meuse and the Rhine. In secret provisions it was agreed that if France retained that occupied territory when general peace was made with the Empire, then Prussia would obtain suitable compensation elsewhere within the Holy Roman Empire. Although nowhere explicitly stated, it was tacitly understood that compensation should be at the expense of the remaining ecclesiastical states which would be secularized. For Prussia the Peace of Basel brought military, political, and economic advantages of enormous worth, not the least of which was the opportunity to share in the Third Partition of Poland. For France the peace was a turning point: the revolutionary idealism of 1792-1793 and the crusade to liberate enslaved peoples had given way to the more old-fashioned interests of state.

Bourbon Spain also made peace, granting full recognition to the conquering Republic. Although it had expected better, Holland, too, was forced to sign a dictated peace, its reorganized republican government agreeing to pay a heavy war indemnity, cede strategic territory in Flanders, open most of the Scheldt to French shipping, support an army of occupation, and contract a defensive and offensive alliance with France. The lesser states, such as Tuscany, Saxony, Hesse-Cassel, and Hanover in their turn bowed to military necessity and made peace on such terms as they could obtain. Only England and Austria of the original members of the First Coalition were left in the field. But the Thermidorian Convention which had broken up the Coalition and had won widespread official recognition for revolutionary and regicide France bequeathed many problems as well as triumphs to the government of the Directory which was to follow it. At home bankruptcy impended. Abroad there was still war with Austria and England; in the coerced and occupied neighboring states there was disillusionment and resentment against the liberators. The Convention also bequeathed political hatreds to its successor.

After the deputies had quelled the insurrection of 1795, they officially prohibited the use of the term "revolutionary" and then hastily drew up the Constitution of the Year III to replace the stillborn Montagnard Constitution of 1793. All was of a piece in this new document: There were tax qualifications for voters and high property requirements for secondary electors. There was a system of indirect elections. The Constitution established a bicameral assembly: an upper house called the Council of Ancients and a lower chamber called the Council of Five Hundred. Finally, there was to be an executive panel of a Directory of five members named by the deputies. According to the calculations of the constitution-makers they were striking a skilful balance between forces and interests potentially antagonistic to each other and disruptive of the security of all. Even the new Declaration of Rights balanced the rights of man with his duties.

Unhappily, these precautions to avert future disturbances and prevent any repetition of radical dictatorship were only too well made. The new charter, lacking all effective provision for the mediation of disputes between the legislative and the executive, and deficient in terms for a speedy revision, was to lead not to balance and harmony, but to drift and disorder, ultimately to dictatorship.

The constitution itself was ratified in a popular referendum. But the plebiscite rejected a rider which the deputies had attached to the constitutional text, supplementary decrees which provided that at least two-thirds of the 750 deputies of the new chambers had to be elected (or co-opted if need be) from among the old members of the Convention. The city of Paris in fact did more than refuse approval of the supplementary decrees. The Conventionals, moderates as most of them were and opposed as they were to the mood of 1793, were preoccupied with their own security, hoping to find it in parliamentary immunity. They totally underestimated the intensity of feeling against them in the wealthier, conservative sections of the capital. Spearheaded by royalists, who played up their fears, these sections rose up in arms to forestall the elections. Had they succeeded, the Republic would have succumbed. They did not succeed. A young captain of artillery, Napoleon Bonaparte, entered into history by turning his cannon on the insurgents of the 13th Vendémiaire (October 5, 1795).

The elections were held as scheduled. Before it met for the last time on October 26, the Convention formally reaffirmed that the revolutionary land sales were valid, thus reassuring its peasant supporters. To placate the enemies of the Revolution, it also voted an amnesty to all opponents except émigrés, refractory clergy, and the leaders of Vendémiaire. The "revolutionary government" was legally terminated; the constitutional government of proprietors was about to begin.

France and the Western World, 1792-1795. Existing fears of the Revolution swelled and deepened outside France after the establishment of the Republic. Preachers and teachers, most of them, were making common cause with émigrés and native conservatives in denouncing the sophisticated cannibals in Paris. Righteously irate, they energetically excommunicated from the universe of the civilized the Jacobin terrorists who, after over-throwing the monarchy and guillotining their king, were now bludgeoning and coercing their compatriots into obedience. As the news of Jacobin infamy moved farther and farther away from the revolutionary scene where some check on veracity could be made, the denunciations grew more unbridled and the distortions took on epic proportions.

In Russia the dying Catherine displayed a petty, per-secuting hostility to France which bordered on the psycho-pathological. Whatever there was once of liberalism in the tsarina whose praises Voltaire had sung for a con-sideration was now burnt out; and she glowed in the expiring fires of her vitality with a neurotic hatred of the followers of the philosophes whom in more robust days she had professed to admire.

Time had been, too, in the Danubian kingdom of the Hapsburgs when the monarchy was progressive. All was now changed in Vienna under Joseph II's nephew, the devout, the timid, and the not very bright Francis II. The landed aristocracy regained its ascendancy over the peasantry; the state, over individual subjects; and the Church, over the state. Of course, ferment had not ended among the racial minorities: Magyars in Hungary, Poles in Galicia, Slavs in Carinthia and Styria, and a handful of courageous individuals—intellectuals, officers, and bureaucrats—in Vienna and Budapest for a time dared carry on correspondence with the French and distribute prorevolutionary literature. Otherwise, silence and res-ignation to the intellectual counter-revolution prevailed in Austria and elsewhere in the Empire. Protests were stifled, as student clubs were closed and lecture halls opened to government spies. The secrecy of the mail was violated, informers took notes on private conversations in inns and coffee houses, and the government condemned to death the misguided liberals who looked to France for inspiration.

In Spain, too, the retreat into the Old Regime was on. French sympathizers were muzzled and pro-French of-ficials dismissed or frightened into outward acceptance

of the government attitude, while the French colony repudiated, willy-nilly, their compatriots in Paris. The
sanitary cordon along the frontier, which had been put
up in 1791, was still maintained. In Spain, as in Prussia,
the war with France was not popular. In Spain, too, the
ally against France, England, was not popular, for the
price of Pitt's aid came high. Further east in the Italies
there was widespread tension, and in Piedmont the political tension threatened to assume revolutionary character.
By themselves the Italian malcontents could do little or
nothing. Not until General Bonaparte's ragamuffins won
their spectacular victories in 1796 could hatred of the
Austrians blend with enthusiasm for the French Revolution to spur the natives into their own revolutionary war
of independence.

The impact of revolutionary France was most immediate and great along her eastern frontier. So much so,
that contemporaries, in the main the learned rather than
the untutored, were firmly convinced that the revolutionaries at Paris had organized a highly ramified conspiracy to undermine existing governments and the social
order. Actually, the belief had little to warrant it. Official
representatives were naturally instructed to make friends
and influence public opinion. They made no secret of
what they were doing, no more than did the soldiers and
the representatives-on-mission who accompanied the
liberators in Belgium and the Rhineland, and in Holland,
too, beyond the natural frontiers. The secret of the penetration of revolutionary ideas was simplicity itself. Wherever peasants groaned under the obligations of the
manorial regime, or rurals and townsmen were crushed
under the weight of taxation, wherever governments were
hated and the privileged classes detested, there French
ideas were made welcome.

Conceivably, if the governing classes had not been
the prisoners of their fears and swayed by the precedents
and objectives of balance-of-power politics, monarchical-
aristocratic Europe could have rolled back the advancing
French. Only belatedly, however, did they come to under-
stand that ideas and aspirations were weapons, too. Because each state mistrusted its ally, because within each
state the ruler feared his own subjects almost as much

as he did the enemy soldiery, the powers could neither form a European Committee of Public Safety nor call for a levy-in-mass at home. The outmoded tactics and weapons with which they fought the French and their absence of vision for the future were staggering.

Among the peoples of Belgium and the small German principalities on the left bank of the Rhine between the Rhine itself and the Meuse, a predisposition had existed to welcome the French troops. After their first crusade to liberate enslaved people, the French had been driven out from that territory. When they reconquered it in 1794 and 1795, their pristine propagandist, missionary fervor was gone. There was no problem with liberated natives in Savoy and Nice which had been annexed since 1792. Belgium was not formally incorporated into France until October 1795, while the Rhenish states did not become part of France, even though long occupied, until 1799. So the new tough and realistic instructions applied primarily to Belgium and the Rhineland and secondarily to Holland, which the French overran early in 1795.

The countries, so ran the instructions, were to be treated like conquered states. Officers and civil commissioners were to prevent fraternizing and break up political gatherings. They were to take from the former government all that France needed of food, clothing, and materiel. They were to introduce the assignat and carry off metallic currency as war indemnity or costs of occupation. They were also to confiscate the property of the Church and the landed aristocracy. If procedure followed a classical pattern of conquest and exploitation, there was a difference: it was the rich and the powerful who were being penalized and expropriated and the poor and the humble who were favored by the new deal. After "the inhabitants," so one set of instructions for Belgium was phrased, "had shown themselves worthy of it by their sacrifices for the defense of liberty," their land would be incorporated with France and they would be entitled as French citizens to all the benefits that the French people had already gained. Meantime their own native officials whom the French had nominated to office cooperated with the Gallic liberators in abolishing the feudal regime and nationalizing the Church property. They cooperated, of course, with the French in systematically exploiting their country and graciously tolerating the preference of their compatriots for the Catholic religion.

The game was not without danger, even fatality, for very soon even the humble and poor tired of French occupying troops, whose personnel was methodically renewed, and of French civil agents. More than one French report to Paris pointed out how likely was the danger of a national uprising should the French forces ever suffer military defeat. Not for some years after the annexation of that territory and its incorporation into France did the worst rigors of liberation end. Nevertheless, no matter how deep their aversion for the ubiquitous French carpet-baggers, the natives never gave up the reforms which jointly with the French soldiers their own revolutionary leaders had carried out.

Great Britain.   In England, conservative opposition to the Revolution in France was hardening fast when the country went to war. More than one liberal was already finding it prudent to keep his political convictions strictly to himself. By mid-1793, public opinion was running so high against the old French enemy that the notorious judge, Lord Braxfield, was on safe emotional ground in whispering to one of the jurors, in a case over which he presided, to help him hang "one of those damned scoundrels" accused of the crime of spreading Paine's work and thus inciting to sedition. The scoundrel in question, a progressive Scots attorney, was not hanged; he was merely sentenced to 14 years' imprisonment in a penal colony.

Of all the political clubs which were under fire, the London Corresponding Society stuck most resolutely to its guns, sponsoring a broad campaign of petitions to compel Parliament to make reforms. The effort failed, and Pitt emerged victorious from a full debate over reforms in Commons. At this time one of the new leaders of the Corresponding Society, a naturalized Frenchman named Maurice Margot, conceived the dramatic but dangerous plan of holding a Convention of democratic delegates from all over the United Kingdom. The name "Convention" was ominous in itself, and Pitt did not delay in his response to this move to put popular pressure upon the government. He ordered the meeting

dispersed by force and the leaders arrested and brought
to trial for sedition. Again Judge Braxfield was in charge,
instructing the jury to regard as sedition the poisoning
of minds and the creation of dissatisfaction. In these
circumstances Margot had no chance: he received a
penalty of deportation and imprisonment at Botany Bay
in Australia. (*See Reading 11, No. I B.*)

By 1794 the patriotic mobs were in an ugly mood. It
was not Coleridge alone who noted that there was not a
city or town in Great Britain where a man suspected of
entertaining democratic sympathies could move without
being unpleasantly reminded of the hatred in which the
majority of the people held his political opinions. It took
courage for the London Corresponding Society to protest
the arrest and trial of its leaders, Hardy and Tooke. (*See
Reading 11, No. I C.*) It took courage, skill, and inspired
eloquence for Thomas Erskine to win their acquittal of
the charge of conspiracy to overthrow the government.
Pitt nevertheless had the final word; between the indictment of the men and their trial, he asked for and secured
the temporary suspension of Habeas Corpus. The year
ended with the cause for reform dead and hysterical
antiforeignism sweeping the home of Magna Charta and
the "Bloodless Revolution."

United States. All the disturbing development that
was sending European conservatives into paroxysms of
fear also alarmed their counterparts in the United States.
Predisposed to dislike and fear France, the Federalists
were agreed with the British ambassador who reported
home to London that "the pernicious principles of the
French Revolution have found here a soil adapted to
their reception." They were determined not to allow the
French alliance of 1778 to be so interpreted as to involve
the United States in difficulties with Great Britain, let
alone in a war against a nation with whom they enjoyed
favorable trade relations and with whom they were
joined by political sympathy. They would not permit the
shocking example of the dangers in France to be emulated in America.

The Republicans, for their part, were persuaded that
the defense of democracy at home was indissolubly
bound with the course of the French Republic abroad.

(*See Reading 11, No. II A.*) Whether or not the United States was to be actually swept into the gigantic struggle overseas, it was in a sense already a participant. Should democracy fail in France and the despots emerge the victors, then the struggle for popular sovereignty would be seriously compromised on their own shores.

To defend this course, democratic and republican societies were founded, eleven in 1793 and twenty-four in 1794. Neither secret nor conspiratorial, they enrolled men from the same social levels from which the Jacobins in France and the political clubs in Britain were drawing their members. Mechanics and artisans, farmers, clerks, and shopkeepers were in the majority, but intellectuals and stout merchants were also in their midst. If on a larger canvas these political clubs formed part of a broad world movement of protest against privilege, on a more restricted plane they were a vigorously authentic expression of Americanism, of a resurgent American faith in democracy. (*See Reading 11, No. II B.*)

In consequence of this array of forces, every policy decision of the government from 1793 on became an issue of partisan politics. Washington's Proclamation of Neutrality in the spring of 1793, which was a clear instance of government determination not to be drawn into the struggle by virtue of the 1778 alliance treaty with France, drew the fire of the Republicans. Neutrality or no, the British continued openly to violate American rights, seize their ships on the high seas, impress their crews, prevent American trade with the recently opened French West Indies, and condemn American cargoes in prize courts.

The curious activities of "Citizen" Genêt, the French Republic's first minister to the United States, also divided the nation. On the one side were the merchants, financiers, and other Americans who believed they could do business with Britain. Behind them stood the commanding figure of George Washington himself, irritated not a little by Genêt's arrogant tactlessness and the outfitting of French privateers in American ports, and properly indignant at Genêt's appeal over his head to American public opinion. Genêt, on the other hand, had enthusiastic supporters; and as he made his way to Philadelphia to be received with icy coolness by President Washington, the crowds greeted him with acclaim. (*See Reading 11, No. II C.*) Freneau reserved for the unfeeling President some of his sharpest barbs and the democratic societies continued to endorse the undiplomatic diplomat. Before the year ended, however, the United States had asked for his recall. The *affaire Genêt* was over.

While his disgrace only temporarily eased the tension between the two governments, it marked the moment when public opinion first veered against the French republicans. Madison's resolution in the House early in 1794 for retaliatory measures against the British furnished the next occasion for political controversy. The Federalists, realizing that its passage could lead the country to war, closed ranks and rallied their supporters to defeat it. The republican societies, with not less ardor, put pressure on Congress to vote it. After spirited debates, the resolution was lost, a temporary embargo being voted instead. But by their intemperate tone during the controversy inside and outside the halls of the assembly, as well as by the vote itself, the democrats yielded additional ground.

Their retreat quickened later that same year, when the government crushed the Whisky Rebellion in the western counties of Pennsylvania. The details of the varied grievances which made that vast region, ranging from western Pennsylvania south to Georgia and west to Kentucky and Tennessee, a cauldron of hatred belong to the history of the United States. What was common to all the sections was the combination of their hatred of England and their love for France with their militant republicanism and their adherence to the democratic societies. When the federal authorities suppressed the rebellion and Washington in wrath characterized the societies' support of the rebels as "the most diabolical attempt to destroy the best fabric of human government and happiness that has ever presented itself for the acceptance of mankind," the friends of France had again given way to the force of public opinion.

Most of all, the Francophiles gave way after the uproar caused by the Jay Treaty. In view of the unsatisfactory relations with Britain, the embargo notwithstanding, and to avoid a war which could be disastrous to the new nation, the Federalists succeeded in having Justice John Jay sent to London to negotiate a general settlement. The aristocratic Jay, whose liking for France was the least pronounced of his characteristics, left amid democratic protest and negotiated a treaty in an atmosphere of secrecy. There is no doubt that the treaty, while highly favorable to Britain and a virtual repudiation of the French alliance, was the best that could be hoped for. But the circumstances attending its secret ratification in the Senate provoked a storm. The terms were leaked to the press, and a passionate debate rocked the country at the very moment that President Washington was making up his mind whether he would or would not sign it.

There were street demonstrations and mass meetings for and against. Jay was defended as a wise patriot. He was also hanged in effigy and denounced as an "illegitimate imp," who had made America "a party to the conspiracy of despots." Nonetheless, President Washington signed the treaty in August 1795, and the House of Representatives voted appropriations the following spring. Once more Washington denounced the societies; again the clergy joined in the chorus of condemnation; more and more Americans yielded to a growing apprehension that a minority of their own countrymen were bent on destroying the social order and endangering liberty. The road lay straight from the apprehensions of 1795-1796 to the Alien and Sedition Acts and the nativist hysteria of 1798-1799. (*See Reading 11, No. II E.*)

— 6 —

THE CONSTITUTIONAL REPUBLIC, 1795-1799

The Government of Proprietors. The new constitutional regime rested upon the most narrow social base. The right to vote was accorded to all Frenchmen aged twenty-one or over who paid a direct tax, but the actual nomination of the deputies and the key administrators was in the hands of secondary electors who were all either owners or tenants of urban or rural property. As one of the deputies who framed the provisions explained, "A country governed by proprietors falls within the social order; one governed by nonproprietors is in the state of nature." The regime was fraudulent from the outset as well as oligarchic: 500 of the 750 deputies had been imposed upon the two Councils by the provisions of the Two-Thirds Decree. Some of these ex-Conventionals were Montagnards and a greater number were right wing Thermidorian republicans. They all favored a sacred union of middle-of-the-road revolutionaries which would bar the way to both a royalist restoration and a new democratic dictatorship. With one exception, also, the five Directors shared with the deputies their desire to pursue a moderate course and consolidate gains that were already made. (*See Reading 12, No. I.*)

The people, weary after years of strain and exertion, yearned like the government for peace and security. The enemies of the Republic gave it neither. Even though General Hoche's columns could crush royalist insurrection in the Vendée and Brittany, the Count of Provence, now styling himself Louis XVIII (the Dauphin who died in prison would have been Louis XVII) still had thousands of secret adherents. Nor was the enemy from the Left inactive. The working masses had profound grievances in this bitter winter of 1795-1796, the most severe of the entire century. Markets were empty of food. Bread, which in the great crisis of 1788-1789 had soared to four sous a pound, could now be had only for seven. Private profiteering was heartless, official corruption scandalous. An idealistic ex-Jacobin who called himself in emulation of the Roman agrarian reformer, "Gracchus" Babeuf, took the lead in organizing the Society of Equals, a secret group of plotters who planned to overthrow the government and take over power. Babeuf himself, in his curious doctrine blended of petty bourgeois Jacobinism and eighteenth-century utopian communism, was convinced that he had formulated a solution to the problem of man's exploitation of man. (*See Reading 12, No. II.*) But his "Conspiracy of Equals," of which later, more scientifically-minded Communists spoke highly, was crushed without difficulty by the police; and a year later, early in 1797, after public opinion had been sufficiently prepared, Babeuf and his chief associates were guillotined.

The government's victory was a Pyrrhic one. By smashing the working-class movement of the Left without giving substantial satisfaction to grievances of the workers, it upset the political balance of the country. It lost its actual or potential democratic supporters and strengthened out of all proportion the conservative opponents who carried on a vigorous pre-electoral campaign on the eve of the first general election. In the spring of 1797 there was open talk of overthrowing the Republic and much secret activity by Anglo-royalist plotters to that end. In fact, antirepublican expectations seemed wholly justified by the results of the election, which was a decisive defeat for the Republicans and a landslide victory for the Right. The election swept some 150 former Conventionals back into private life and returned to the Councils a great number of constitutional monarchists together with some out-and-out Old Regime royalists. With a restoration impending, émigrés began to slip across the frontier from Italy and the Rhineland, while refractory priests conducted services, almost openly in defiance of the authorities.

The royalists were too sanguine, not least the would-be Louis XVIII who publicly announced his intention to restore the Old Regime and visit dire punishment upon all revolutionists without distinction. For the next several months the antirepublican wave mounted steadily, and in mid-summer the frightened deputies sent a final despairing appeal for help to the field commanders in the eastern theater and in north Italy. At this point the royalist leaders in the two Councils initiated indictment proceedings against three republican Directors, hoping in this way to obtain immediate control of the executive and to confront the republicans with an accomplished fact. The miraculously victorious General Bonaparte did not let the appeals go unheeded. From his headquarters in northern Italy, where he was holding court while negotiating with the defeated Austrians, he despatched a subordinate commander, General Augereau, to Paris. Augereau lost no time in taking over military command of the capital on the 18th of Fructidor (September 4, 1797) and in arresting the royalist leaders in the Councils. He then issued a proclamation threatening to shoot without trial anyone who advocated either a royalist restoration or the adoption of the Jacobin Constitution of 1793.

Paris remained quiet. Under the protecting bayonets of the grenadiers, the Councils canceled the election of almost 200 deputies and purged the Directory of its royalist members. They saved the Republic by this violation of the constitution, but for two years after the coup of Fructidor, the Republic lived on under the veritable dictatorship of the Directory. In 1797 the Directors revived punitive legislation against émigrés and priests, arresting political leaders, shooting them, or deporting them to the penal colonies. A year later they nullified the elections again, which this time went to the Left, and again employed the cold guillotine of deportation to outstanding opposition leaders.

The coup of Fructidor reacted decisively on the foreign relations of the Republic as well as upon its domestic evolution. Dependent though the Directory was upon the victorious generals who were sending back wagonloads of booty and plunder to Paris, no one in the government seriously entertained the thought that France would retain the conquests that the field commanders had made beyond the natural frontiers of the Rhine and the Alps. Almost everyone, on the contrary, looked forward to utilizing those victories in order to speed Austria's withdrawal from the war by giving her territorial compensation for the loss of Belgium. With Austria out, they reasoned, England would then be compelled to sue for peace; and to Pitt also, the Directory was prepared to give territory, territory overseas, in return for England's recognition up to the line of the natural frontiers.

Fate, in the person of Napoleon Bonaparte, upset those calculations. Living off his booty, independent of the Paris civil authorities through his spectacular conquests in northern Italy, Bonaparte not only upset the military plans of the Directory, but by defying instructions he also upset its diplomacy. Part of his grand design he disclosed in the preliminary negotiations and agreements with Austria in the spring of 1797. Other aspects which he did not then dare to disclose came to light later, for after Fructidor the Directory was almost wholly incapable of balking his diplomacy.

The treaty of Campo Formio (October 17, 1797) which established peace on the continent was a major diplomatic triumph for the revolutionary republic. Even more was it a personal triumph for Bonaparte. It was an imperialistic peace. To win Austrian assent to the loss of Belgium and the establishment of the nominally independent Cisalpine Republic in northern Italy, Bonaparte turned over to the Emperor most of the territory of the once independent Republic of Venice, which he had invaded and conquered under the flimsiest of pretexts for intervention. With his own eastern schemes in mind, Bonaparte obtained for France the former Venetian-controlled Ionian Islands, along with considerable territory on the eastern shore of the Adriatic. And to win the Emperor's endorsement of the French acquisition of the left bank, Bonaparte agreed in secret articles to use the "good offices" of France to aid Austria in acquiring compensation within Germany. In short, France would intervene in the internal affairs of the Empire, this time in behalf of Austria, rather than in behalf of Prussia as the similarly secret provisions of the Treaty of Basel had called for.

Fructidor also played a decisive part in the current peace negotiations with England. While the first conversations of 1796 had failed, the summer talks of 1797 at Lille were more promising, and a tentative understanding in fact was reached on the eve of the coup, whereby in return for the French retention of Belgium, England would be compensated by the cession of Ceylon, the Cape of Good Hope, and Trinidad. France, it will be noted, was as quick in making gifts of the territory of her allies as she was in acquiring for herself the territory of her enemies. Then came Fructidor and the French negotiators at once raised their terms. The British would not agree and the conference broke up in failure. For more than a year until the end of 1798 Britain stood alone in Europe, girding herself for invasion and marshalling what new resources she could of men, money, and materiel against the economic warfare that the enemy was waging.

The invasion did not come, Bonaparte willing it otherwise; and at the end of the year Britain no longer stood alone. Bonaparte was himself in the East seeking glory and the opportunity to bring England to her knees by conquering Egypt, cutting a canal through the Isthmus of Suez, and marching his troops to India. A new general war broke out in his absence and a Second Coalition of powers—England, Austria, Russia, the Ottoman Empire, and Naples—was in the field to block new French diplomatic and military aggression. For on the continent the Directory took advantage of its enormous increase in strength and prestige to try and reshape the face of Europe. Upon the technically independent Batavian Republic the French occupants imposed a new constitutional charter, modeled after the "Fructidorized" Directory in Paris. The Swiss cantons were reorganized into the centralized Helvetic Republic. The pope was made prisoner and a Roman Republic came into being. The Kingdom of Naples, after its occupation, was also transformed into a sister republic, the Parthenopean Republic.

Many considerations, including the Republic's determination to gain security for the newly-annexed territory, entered into the rush upon Europe. Security, however, was not won, for the initial fighting went disastrously against the French. Nelson's fleet cut off the French army in Egypt and made Bonaparte a prisoner for all practical purposes in the land that he had conquered. The situation was even worse in Europe. The Russians overran Switzerland and an Anglo-Russian expeditionary force landed in Holland. The defenses of the Cisalpine Republic crumbled and all the rest of Italy, excepting Genoa alone, was also lost to the enemy. In France, where a majority of radical republican deputies was returned to the lower chamber in the spring elections of 1799, the political pendulum swung far to the Left. The new deputies placed the odium for the military reverses and the economic distress upon the Directors and at once purged the discredited executive branch of the government. Four new Directors took office in consequence of that coup of Prairial, all but one of them sympathetic in outlook to the enactment of emergency measures and to the establishment of a new Jacobin dictatorship to save the threatened fatherland.

The unfrocked Abbé Sieyès was among the members of the new Directory, recently emerged from long political obscurity and now pressing his plans for the revision of the much battered and violated Constitution. Although he had accepted nomination from the leftist deputies, his views on government were not theirs. His constitutional formula fell considerably short of democracy: it called for confidence from below, while authority or power was to come from above. He had among the Directors only one supporter for his views, but in the Council of Ancients most of the deputies were behind him. The task as he conceived it was to roll back the Jacobin tide, surmount the danger from the royalists whose hopes the military defeats of their compatriots had raised, and find an accommodating general who would keep law and order pending the peaceful revision of the constitution.

The danger from the royalist side evaporated by itself, for during the summer of 1799 the war turned suddenly in favor of the French. The brilliant victories of Masséna in Italy and Brune in Holland again made the French frontiers secure. With the invasion danger over and the immediate royalist threat ended, Sieyès turned his attention to the Jacobins. Ably seconded by the ex-Terrorist Fouché, now minister of police, he succeeded in having most of the emergency revolutionary measures rescinded so that the *patrie* was already saved in October 1799, when General Bonaparte unexpectedly landed on the shores of southern France.

The crisis was over, as Bonaparte was making his triumphal way to Paris, but the apprehensions reawakened by the Jacobin emergency measures still remained. It required little effort on the part of Sieyès to convince the moneyed interests and the deputies whose memories of the Terror Government were vivid that a new Jacobin menace hung over them. Bonaparte with whom he established contact was also willing to be persuaded, affecting to believe in the reality of a Jacobin plot to overthrow the Directory. After taking his bearings with different political groups he agreed to lend his sword to Sieyès in order to save the country. Upon the sword Sieyès could count; unfortunately for himself he had not reckoned with Bonaparte's lust for power.

The plan was to dissolve the existing government and concentrate emergency authority in the hands of the revisionists. What the coups of Fructidor and Prairial had done in somewhat disguised fashion, Sieyès and Bonaparte would do openly. The arrangements agreed upon, however, almost miscarried between the 18th and the 19th Brumaire, Year VII (November 9 and 10, 1799). In the end Bonaparte's soldiers carried out their assignment: with bayonets drawn they expelled the republican deputies from the assembly halls. A rump council met that same night and appointed a board of three provisional Consuls, Bonaparte among them, to govern France. A commission was then nominated to revise the Constitution, and only three weeks later the new executive officially and formally declared that the Revolution was ended. (*See Reading 12, No. IV.*) Ten years of revolutionary struggle had eventuated in the victory of the military adventurer, a revolutionary adventurer of genius.

France and the Western World, 1795-1799.   There was no abatement of fear in the European states that lay beyond the natural frontiers to which by 1795 France had advanced. Up to the last, in the frozen wastes of the north, Catherine of Russia breathed fire and sword against "the destroyers of thrones and society." When she died, her son Paul ascended the throne, and in hostility to the French Revolution and in persecution of progressives the deranged successor was not appreciably different from his more balanced predecessor. In the Germanies, it was Prussia, benefitting from the security that neutrality bestowed upon her, that relaxed the severity of persecution. Elsewhere, particularly in Vienna, the steady march into reaction continued apace. The bases were being sunk for the future Metternich system.

    Great Britain. The reaction was also in full sway in Great Britain. The campaign of the government against the clubs, as has been noted, closed them all, the London Corresponding Society excepted, while in that same year patriotic mobs clamorously roughed French sympathizers. Curiously enough, in the following year, out of military reverses abroad and a bad harvest at home, there was a passing recrudescence of violence against the government. Hostile demonstrators attempted to pull George III from his carriage as he was on his way to open Parliament. At a mass outdoor protest meeting, frightened Francophobes and patriots jeered and hooted at Pitt and the king, shouting lustily for bread and peace. Riots swept England that year.

    Only too conscious, and it would have been difficult to blink the facts, that the country was inflammable, Pitt took stern action to stamp out the danger. He had enacted the repressive Two Acts, the first of which, the Seditious Meetings Act, made it necessary to obtain special permission from the authorities to hold large indoor public meetings, while the Treasonable Practices Act put criticism as well as actual deeds against the government into the category of treason. After the suspension of Habeas Corpus, thought control and speech control, it seemed, could hardly go further.

    Yet worse repression was to follow. And in fact there was substance for the government's sense of insecurity. Peace negotiations with France broke down in the summer of 1796. The uneasy Pitt was condemned to stand by and watch the French expeditionary force of 15,000 men making ready at Brest to sail for Ireland where Wolfe Tone's United Irishmen stood poised for insurrection the moment General Hoche landed his troops. The year 1797 was no better. Hoche's expedition turned out a bleak failure; failure or no, the Irish insurrectionists erupted in a fierce rebellion, burning and slaying in their fury. In that same terrifying year the long grumbling English sailors broke out in open mutiny, first at Spithead and then at the Nore. The very pillar of stability, the Bank of England, was hard put to it to meet its obligations; and the country went off the gold standard. Sorely beset, Pitt renewed peace negotiations, but the second series of talks at Lille also collapsed. Austria made peace with Bonaparte; for more than a year Britain alone withstood the conqueror, ravaged by her fears.

The reaction, in this most perilous of years, reached its height. Although Pitt's energetic moves broke the threat of the Irish rebellion, not until Bonaparte departed for Egypt did the menace end of a cross-Channel invasion and could Englishmen afford to breathe easily again. Then Pitt turned his attention, supported as before by outraged patriotic mobs, to the crushing of English enemies at home. The fears that he entertained or professed to entertain of native conspirators seem in the absence of supporting evidence quite groundless. The panicky fears that he exploited so systematically were real enough.

His government suppressed the last of the clubs and placed trade unions under a legal ban. To protect the government against criticism, it instituted a severe censorship over the press, even forbidding English newspapers to introduce into their pages foreign material of "dangerous tendency." Once again Habeas Corpus was suspended. As the decade neared its close, the machinery of coercive repression was working smoothly and systematically. A handful of publicists would not be cowed, and intrepid parliamentary critics fought hard and well to save the constitutional liberties of their countrymen. But the reform movement was killed for many years to come. The blind patriotic fervor of the crowds, the forceful activity of the government, and the unmitigated sway of landlords over tenants and laborers, combined to spare England from popular sovereignty and Jacobin democracy.

Ireland. A complex, many-sided agitation was meantime sweeping Ireland. Henry Grattan, the eloquent

Protestant reformer, in the years immediately preceding 1789 had won notable concessions from Whitehall. When the French Revolution burst forth, however, its influence fell upon Ireland where political grievances still rankled, where religious disabilities still obtained, and burning economic inequalities, too. In the first years the Irish malcontents gave enthusiastic welcome to the changes abroad. Those years saw the Irish enemies of England come together, the Presbyterians from Ulster and the Catholic Peep-of-Day Boys, in the Society of United Irishmen. Hopes ran high that somehow, through the pressure of public opinion and a large-scale education effort with the masses, the long-delayed reforms would be enacted.

Irishmen were by 1793 no longer united. In the countryside violence broke out again and the peasants were on the prowl, looting the manor houses and burning hayricks. Religious strife, ill-contained for several years, again pitted Catholics against Protestants. Wolf Tone pressed for a rebellion; and in the United Irishmen, fast becoming a semimilitary organization, new leaders like Lord Fitzgerald had come to the fore, determined to stop at nothing short of secession and to effect it, if necessary, by insurrection.

Although General Hoche's troops never landed to give the awaited signal, the insurrection flared up without French cooperation. Both sides fought savagely, the rebels and the troops of the English government, but by mid-1798 the superior government forces had matters well in hand. Upon Pitt devolved the heavy responsibility of bringing peace to an unhappy land, driven by burning nationalist hatred of its conqueror, torn by religious and social strife within. The rumor spread, as hundreds of insurgents lay in English jails, that the government was considering offering them freedom if they agreed to emigrate to the United States. Even if true, the offer would have failed. In 1798 the United States was in no mood to welcome insurrectionists, least of all insurrectionists sympathetic to France.

United States. The reaction was already well under way in the United States when in 1797 a dejected and weary George Washington retired from public life and John

Adams with a divided cabinet and a divided country took over the presidency. Half the country was upbraiding the new President as a war-mongering monarchist and the other castigating Jefferson, the Vice-President, as an atheistic lover of France. War clouds were gathering. Not only had the Directory contemptuously rejected the new American minister, whom it threatened to arrest, but on the high seas the French fleet was stopping American ships and confiscating their cargoes. An unofficial break had already taken place. President Adams urged Congress to strengthen national defense, while old friends, embittered over the issues of foreign policy, crossed the street, Jefferson noted, to avoid speaking to each other.

At this period of stress the fertile intelligence of Alexander Hamilton hit upon the idea of sending a commission of three men to Paris to settle outstanding problems in direct talks, even as Jay had done with England. The intent was laudable, for the two countries were drifting toward war. The plan however went amiss. The three commissioners came to the French capital in October 1797, just when the Directory had broken up the First Coalition, and upon them too the French government practiced its tactics of bribery, coercion, and threats. In time the almost incredible details of the diplomatic incident known as the XYZ Affair, in which the French tried to force the three envoys to pay heavy bribes under pain of war and the fate of ravaged Venice, reached Adams, who officially and apprehensively transmitted them to Congress with a request that they be withheld from the press.

The request was not kept, naturally, for the temptation was well-nigh irresistible to make political capital even at the risk of fanning patriotism into war flames. A terrible uproar ensued, surpassing in intensity and sweep of demonstrations, petitions, altercations, and protests, everything that America had known before of anti-French feeling. A real, undeclared war was on with France, and true battles were fought on the high seas. Almost at once, the fine Italian hand of Talleyrand, in full control now of French foreign affairs, was felt. With dexterity and intelligence he poured oil on troubled feelings and made it possible for Adams, without unduly weakening the American position, to renew negotiations and eventually in 1800 send a second and successful mission to Paris.

Those delicate negotiations were conducted privately, unknown to the general American public, whom rumors, denunciations, and contagious fears brought to the brink of hysteria. It was in a witches' nightmare of belief that thousands of hostile French aliens, aided and abetted by native American democratic Jacobins, had organized a conspiracy against the government that Congress passed and Adams signed the series of Alien and Sedition Acts of 1798, which brought America close to civil war and dissolution. The wisest commentary ever made on these acts was uttered by Madison: "Perhaps it is a universal truth that the loss of liberty at home is to be charged to provisions against danger real or pretended from abroad."

The frenzy that gripped America in 1798 and 1799 was neither more justifiable nor less than the similar madness which prevailed in England. The Alien Act empowering the President temporarily to deport aliens either held dangerous to the public peace and safety or suspected of treasonable and secret machinations was constitutional enough if ill-advised. If this measure was aimed at Irish immigrants as well as French aliens, the second act, the Sedition Act, which was designed in large part to coerce the republican press on the eve of the presidential election of 1800, was neither constitutional nor wise. There was keen opposition in Congress to the provisions which made libelous and defamatory remarks and criticism of members of the government a criminal offense punishable in federal courts; opposition also for similar provisions concerning utterances calculated to excite "unlawful" combinations contrary to the laws and acts of the President. But with the Federalist press, congressmen, and private individuals deliberately fanning nativist hatreds and with the judiciary utterly partisan, there was little that defenders of civil liberties like Madison and Jefferson could do, the Kentucky and Virginia Resolutions apart, save count upon time. (*See Reading 11, No. II D.*)

Time served them faster than they could have hoped. The elections of 1800, which brought Jefferson to the presidency, repudiated the mood of 1798-1799 and made it clear that Americans still believed in popular sovereignty and government of the people. In England the French Revolution had revived political clubs and agitation for reform, but it effected no change in government. In the United States the great debate benefitted democracy more: it educated the common man in national politics and it exposed the aristocratic bias of the Federalist leaders to whom the American republic was so indebted in the first decade of its existence.

The Areas Close to France. In that part of Europe which lay closest to France, the guiding impulse had been in 1792-1793 to liberate the enslaved peoples. After the break-up of the Coalition, when civilians and generals alike were imbued with the consciousness of their country as *la grande nation,* superior as well as victorious and entitled by the laws of nature to the natural frontiers that her armies had gained, the accent fell heavily upon France and French national interests. In consequence the people of the annexed and incorporated territory continued as before to pay for benefits received. The privileged aristocracy, both lay and secular, had been dispossessed by 1799; the feudal and manorial regimes, totally uprooted. The sale of nationalized property was proceeding briskly. Careers were open, within the salutary limitations imposed by the occupying liberators, to the talents of the home population. To be sure, old grievances still rankled: omnipresent French civil and military officials, periodic requisitions of food and materiel, military service obligations, and sporadic religious persecution. But the people were free, practicing more or less popular sovereignty. Time, the great healer, was working, aided by his assistant, the pocketbook, to reconcile the old with the new.

The French armies also extended their conquests beyond the natural frontiers and set up new sister or satellite republics beyond the lines of the Alps and the Rhine. The bastions in Holland, Switzerland, and the Italian peninsula were designed, in part at least, to give military protection to the newly annexed territory on the French side of the lines. With all those nominally independent and allied republics—the Batavian Republic in Holland; the Helvetic Republic in Switzerland; and in the Italian peninsula, the Cisalpine Republic in the north, the Roman Republic, and the Parthenopean Republic in the south—the pattern of French penetration and collaboration with native revolutionists was much the same.

They were all founded under the protecting arms of the French troops. In all of them either the French field commander or the civil commissar played a leading part in drafting the provisions of the new republican constitution, indeed of the new constitutions, for everywhere the charters were toned down after the coup of Fructidor in Paris in 1797 and conversely amended in a more democratic direction after the changes of Floréal in 1798. In all instances the drive toward revolutionary change came from the native population. Activists plotting revolution were in a small, even insignificant minority; and the great majority gave their authorities little or no trouble. But deeply opposed to their own government and native *privilégiés*, they joined political clubs, openly where possible, secretly where necessary, and they enthusiastically welcomed the invading and liberating French armies.

Their prorevolutionary cast of mind was blended everywhere of several ingredients. At its core there was the old aversion for the regime of privilege and favoritism. Dutch burghers, like the French bourgeoisie of 1789, had had more than enough of the rule of the aristocracy. Among the merchants of Holland, as well as the merchants of Belgium, there was also the old indignation against the new Carthage, against the Britain from whose tyrannical sway over trade and finance revolutionary France would soon emancipate all Europe. And in Italy, where the fires of Anglophobia did not burn, there burned the flame of anti-Austrian feeling and of anti-Bourbon sentiment. Popular sovereignty, national patriotism and resentment of foreign domination were compounded in the temper which predisposed these people to look approvingly upon the French troops.

Without exception, also, in these states, the men who directed the attack upon the old order soon began to disagree among themselves on how far they would carry revolutionary reforms. The pattern of development discloses that the solution of the disagreements rested largely in the hands of the French, here of the generals, there of the civil agents, but in any case of the French. There was to be one road to liberty, the French one; and if the new republics pursued that road, they had the glory of being in charge of their own destiny.

The systematic utilization of the resources of the satellite republics was also part of the pattern. In Holland, both political intimidation and economic exploitation were relatively slight compared to what they might have been, compared to what they were in Switzerland and in the Italies. Of them all it was undoubtedly the Roman Republic which felt most poignantly the misrule of rapacious officers and brutal commissars. In the Parthenopean Republic of Naples the French military defeats in 1799 gave the signal for a sickening white terror against radicals and progressives. In Switzerland, while town oligarchs appeased the new political heads with bribes, in the mountain cantons the Catholic peasantry long maintained dogged resistance. Paradoxically, if not ironically, it was the democratic groups in the Cisalpine Republic which were most at odds with the new government that Bonaparte had set up after the Peace of Campo Formio without either consulting Paris or obtaining popular ratification from the Italians. What those democrats wanted was a united and independent Italy, free of Austrians. Neither Bonaparte nor the Directory had that end in mind. In consequence, although Bonaparte's proclamations encouraged nationalist hopes, his soldiers shot down Italians who voiced them and worked to realize them.

Thus the ledger in 1799 showed revolutionary France in indirect control, if not ruling by open force over the allies upon whom it imposed many obligations. It showed also new institutions, which were to become a permanent legacy to each country. In all those states subjects had been transformed into citizens. Revolutionary France found among those people lasting converts to its liberating principles. To the underprivileged its aid was decisive.

CONCLUSION

FRANCE IN 1799

The victors of Brumaire who officially declared the Revolution ended gave no guarantee that French men and women and children would live to enjoy its benefits. Actually, at that moment, the balance sheet disclosed disheartening setbacks. The end of the war was not in sight. Colonies were cut off or lost; neutrals were reluctant to trade with France; the seas were blockaded and under British control; colonial goods, if available at all, were costly and in short supply.

In Paris Bonaparte's soldiers kept the peace, but in the departments the peace was troubled. Highways were infested with brigands, while organized bands of criminals mocked the efforts of local authorities to maintain law and order. On all sides there was grim evidence of ten years of revolution and civil strife: dilapidated and damaged buildings, defaced churches with their mutilated statues of saints, wretchedly attired citizens, and roads scarred and torn up. In law all Frenchmen enjoyed liberty of conscience and freedom of religious observance. The practice did not square with principle. The several religious groups contended with each other, the long-persecuted refractory clergy showing themselves almost as hostile to the juring clergy as they were to the civil revolutionary authorities. In the west and the south they openly aided the royalist rebels; in all France the faithful made a point of ignoring the revolutionary calendar and civic fetes, persevering stubbornly in celebrating the Christian sabbath and the saints' days.

Though the Directory had gone back to a regime of hard money, much of the scarce metallic currency was in hiding. Industrial production, already badly affected by ten years of disorder, was starved for capital funds. While the disorder and violence made the transport of goods difficult and dangerous within the country, the curtailed international commerce had fallen far below the 1789 figures. Agriculture, like industry, was lagging, technically backward and mired in routine. For all the efforts at economy and all improvements in tax collection, the government revenue was inadequate, inferior to expenditures by 286,000,000 livres in 1799.

The high sense of duty and responsibility, of dedication indeed, which had pulled the revolutionaries through the crisis of the Year II, was all but gone from the hearts of the divided people of 1799. From the Old Regime aristocracy one could not expect civic spirit, nor from the new investors whom the repudiation in 1797 of state indebtedness amounting to almost 2,000,000,000 livres had decimated. The nouveaux riches flaunted the millions gained from profiteering, war contracts, and land speculation, but there was also much suffering and want. In Paris alone there were 90,000 needy unemployed, and in all the other large cities workers were sullen, many of them out of work and the employed complaining about deflationary low wages. There were still many marginal peasants and landless in the rural area, lacking medical care and educational opportunity, demanding poor relief from an impoverished treasury that gave no response.

Still, the Revolution had not failed. Whether necessary or not, the coup of Brumaire was a gamble that paid off for beneficiaries of ten years of change. True that the Napoleonic seizure of power ushered in fifteen years of political authoritarianism at home and military adventure abroad; but when the adventure was ended and the dictatorship repudiated, it was still the middle classes of trade and industry and finance who were in control of the French state and society. The gains of the revolutionary decade were not destroyed. Far more than is dreamed of in the pages of liberal textbooks the bourgeois elites safeguarded their revolutionary achievements.

In 1799 written declarations guaranteed to the individual the rights which he had come to regard as natural —life, liberty, security, and the pursuit of happiness.

Frenchmen were free, in law at least, to speak and discuss and write, and free also to select their careers. They were both free and equal before the judge and the political clerk, before the recruiting officer and the tax collector. Except when reasons of state denied it, which was not infrequent, they were free to worship as they pleased or believed. They were living in a state officially secular and neutral, in a state which had disestablished the Church, giving now no support to any cult. Curtailed or violated many of these rights still were in 1799, yet their formal recognition in written charters was in itself an immense step forward in the long struggle for human freedom.

The winning of these rights had gone together with the destruction of privilege and the abolition of the corporate structure of society. The tithes of the Church were abolished and the Church as a corporate entity had been destroyed. The old elites were dead or in exile or, if alive in France, discredited and impoverished. In the immediate aftermath of war the new social elites counted too many officers and too many grubby war profiteers. But the permanent new elite came from the social aristocracy of the middle classes of the arts and the sciences, the professions and the business world, from the bourgeoisie that had begun the Revolution of 1789.

The Revolution did more than destroy the old fixed social order. It destroyed the complex, confusing, and picturesque inequalities in administration, legal procedure, and the fiscal system. The absolute monarchy of the Old Regime had disappeared for good. The principles of unquestioning political obedience had given place to the ideal of free acceptance. Royal fiat made way for persuasion. To a degree which few people would have held possible in 1789, France was becoming a centralized nation-state with a simple and uniform administrative system that was unparalleled in Europe. Unfortunately for its security, this new France was still challenged by thousands of Frenchmen held fast in loyalty to the old and driven by hatred for the Revolution. A new loyalty, however, was taking hold of millions of Frenchmen. A fierce love for *la patrie* was filling their hearts, an immense pride in the great deeds of *la grande nation*. And not the least powerful of forces remaking France was

the citizen army itself, the million citizen-soldiers, requisitioned and conscripted, shabbily uniformed and poorly
shod, who were to perpetuate in folklore and secular
faith the epic story of their victory over the monarchs
of Europe.

The grievances that men of affairs had voiced in the
cahiers, those, too, the Revolution in large measure
satisfied. It liberated economic enterprise from legal
restrictions and old, needless regulations. It abolished
the guilds and the internal customs boundaries. A system
of uniform weights and measures had been adopted, a
single unit of currency, and one system of taxation for
all. Uniform legal principles and procedures, more and
more, were governing economic enterprise. Under the
new unity and equality the law protected large-scale
enterprise against workers' associations. By tariffs, boun-
ties, and navigation acts, a benevolent government warded
off competition from abroad.

The decade saw the most radical revolution of a thousand years in the status of the peasantry. It liberated
them from the bondage of the manorial regime, leaving
the peasant free to apply to his own land the productive
energy that he had been compelled to put in the service
of the lord of the manor. He now had full title to the
land that he once had only possessed. Many peasants
also bought state land confiscated from the Church, the
crown, or from the émigrés. And on all this land, whether
old or newly acquired, they paid only a direct tax. The
tithe was gone, and gone too were the hated indirect
taxes of evil memory. Not a few peasants were too poor
to take advantage of the sales. Many of them remained
what they had been before 1789, marginal cultivators.
Many, too, were still sharecroppers or completely landless. Nevertheless, the Revolution accelerated the long
historical evolution: a conservative peasant democracy of
small proprietors was in the making.

To the triumphant men of property also went the
educational spoils. The virtual teaching monopoly of
the Church was broken in the early days of the revolutionary struggle when lofty reform projects were drawn
up for national education. Not until late in 1795, in the
closing days of the Thermidorian Convention, however,

did the deputies finally reorganize the educational system. By then revolutionary idealism was well tinctured with fear of popular democracy. The decree made no provision for obligatory attendance in the primary schools, and the children of the working poor whose labor force was needed at home rarely attended them. In any case, the state schools were few and inadequate, and the financially able families sent their children to the better equipped and more numerous private schools.

In theory, youths from the age of twelve to eighteen could enroll in the new public high schools, the remarkable and unfortunately short-lived *écoles centrales*. In reality, educational selection again fortified social selection, for only the well-to-do could afford the considerable expense of having their children attend them. In all these schools, of which there was only one in each department, the instructors were carefully chosen. All were competent and able, some were distinguished and brilliant in their field of research. Instruction was free, except for fees, and secular in spirit. Without neglecting the humanities, the scope was broadened, and the curriculum stressed design and mathematics and, most of all, the sciences.

The financial stringency had starved the budget for poor relief and social welfare. In the circumstances the provisions for higher instruction and specialized studies seem at first sight quite amazing, until one remembers what one should not forget, that the revolutionists came from the cultural elite. In saving what they could of their priceless heritage in the arts and the sciences from irresponsible vandals, they were faithful to the Enlightenment in which they were reared. In refraining from molestation of scientists as scientists and in making as generous provision as circumstances allowed for research, the revolutionists were discharging by an act of faith the debt that they owed to science.

Such glories of nineteenth-century France as the Museum of the Louvre, the National Library (*Bibliothèque Nationale*), and the National Archives were all established by the revolutionary state. The legend notwithstanding, Lavoisier never uttered the remark long attributed to him that the Revolution had no need of scientists. The Ecole Polytechnique was founded during the Terror; the Jardin du Roi was transformed into the remarkable research center of the Museum of Natural History. The years of political upheaval saw the work of Monge, Laplace, and Condorcet in mathematics and physics; of giants like Lamarck, Cuvier, and Saint-Hilaire in botany and zoology; of Lavoisier and Berthollet in chemistry. The Academy of Sciences was abolished but most of its members took their seats in the Institute of France which replaced it. There were no *Académiciens* in the emigration.

The France of 1799, for all those accomplishments, was tired, shabby, and sorely divided. There were many grievances still to satisfy, many new passions to allay. But the foundations of new France had been laid, and time was to show how remarkably solid they were. Between republican France and monarchical Europe there was in this last year of the expiring century no iron curtain. The fallout of the great explosion in France spread widely over Europe and the Americas, and for several generations. The revolutionary decade was long remembered as the ten years that shook the world.

Part II

READINGS

— Reading No. 1 —

THE CREED OF THE BOURGEOISIE [1]

The different interpretations of the influence of the "philosophers" and the reasons for the wide acceptance of their doctrines are well brought out in the following passages. The first is from a public lecture given in 1912 by Augustin Cochin, an outstanding Catholic and conservative historian; the second comes from the last published work of the late Philippe Sagnac, a distinguished historian of the liberal, secular, and prorevolutionary school.

✓   ✓   ✓

I. The *Philosophes:* A Hostile View

. . . What is *"la philosophie?"* A sect, one usually says: and indeed it is one to all outward appearance.

Orthodoxy, to begin with: "Reason," writes Diderot in the *Encyclopedia,* "is to the *philosophe* what grace is to the Christian." This is the principle of our freethinkers: "We have faith in reason." Thus what one asks of the brethren is less to serve reason than to believe in it. This is just as true of that cult as it is of any other: it is good will that saves. "There are *philosophes,"* says Voltaire, "even in the stalls." . . . And d'Alembert writes to Frederick II in 1776: "We fill the vacant seats in the

[1] These two excerpts are translated from the French: (I), from A. Cochin, *Les sociétés de pensée et la démocratie,* 5th ed. (Paris, 1921), pp. 3-7; (II), from P. Sagnac, *La formation de la société française moderne,* II (Paris, 1946), pp. 298-299.

Academy as we can, in much the same way as they were filled at the feast . . . in the Gospel—with the lame and the halt of literature." Such and such a warped mind will be admitted, if he is a good *philosophe,* and such and such another kept out who is strong but independent. . . .

Demanding on the score of orthodoxy, "philosophy" is no less so on discipline. Voltaire never stops preaching union to the brethren: "I wish that the *philosophes* could become a corps of initiates, then J would die content," he writes to d'Alembert; and again in 1758: "Get together and you will be the masters; I speak to you as a republican but the republic of letters is at stake. O poor republic." These prayers of "the Patriarch" were both answered and surpassed from 1770 on. The republic of letters was founded, organized, and armed, and it intimidated the court. It had its legislators, the *Encyclopedia;* its parlement, two or three salons; its tribunal, the French Academy, where Duclos introduced "philosophy" and d'Alembert insured its rule after fifteen years of uninterrupted, persevering struggle. It had, especially in the provinces, its colonies and outlets. There were academies in the large cities where, as at the Mazarin Palace [*seat of the French Academy*], *philosophes* and independents are at odds and where the latter are always vanquished; literary societies and reading rooms in the small cities; and from one end to the other of this vast network of societies there is an endless exchange of correspondence, addresses, petitions, motions, an immense concert of words; a wonderful harmony with not a discordant note. The army of "philosophers" is dispersed throughout the land, where each city has its garrison of thinkers, its "center of enlightenment." They drill everywhere in the same spirit, according to the same methods, in the same verbal labor of platonic discussions. From time to time, at a signal from Paris, they assemble for grand maneuvers, "affairs," as they already called them, judicial or political incidents; and they are up in arms against the clergy, against the court, indeed, against any unwary private individual. . . .

For they persecute—another sectarian practice. Before the bloody Terror of 1793, there was, from 1765 to 1780, in the republic of letters, a dry terror, of which the *En-*

cyclopedia was the Committee of Public Safety and d'Alembert the Robespierre. It mowed down reputations as the other did heads; its guillotine was defamation, holding up to infamy, as they called it. The phrase, launched by Voltaire, was used in 1775 in the provincial societies with legal precision. To "hold up to infamy" is a well-defined operation which involves a regular procedure: inquest, discussion, ruling, finally execution of the verdict; in short, public condemnation to scorn, another one of those terms of philosophical law whose meaning we no longer appreciate. And heads fall in great numbers. . . .

There, you see, is the whole outward appearance of a vigorous and well-armed sect, sufficient to defeat the enemy, sufficient also to arouse the curiosity of onlookers, such as we are this evening; because behind such high walls, we must expect to find a big city, even a beautiful cathedral; one does not conceive, in general, of fanaticism without faith, or discipline without loyalty, of excommunication without communion, of anathemas without powerful and living convictions—any more than one can conceive of a body without a soul.

But here is the wonder of it; here and only here, are we mistaken: this powerful apparatus of defense defends nothing, nothing but a void and a negation. There is nothing behind it to love, nothing to hold on to and to attach oneself to. This dogmatic reason is only the negation of all faith, this tyrannical liberty, the negation of all restraint. I do not stress a reproach so often made about the *philosophes*: that they themselves avow and glorify the nihilism of their own ideal. . . .

II. A Defense of the Liberal Doctrine

With the fusion of the different elements a complex state of mind was created, neither English nor American, neither purely rationalist nor classic, nor exclusively empiricist, but blended of all of them. . . . But beyond this blend, supporting it, animating it, giving it movement and life, there is a powerful sentiment which invests it with boundless strength—a strength like religion itself— and that is faith in the "regeneration" of French society. Regeneration first of each Frenchman, "the resurrection of Frenchmen as men," as André Chénier said, and "as citizens," and then of all citizens into a "nation." It is an act of faith, of the will. Through it, the synthesis of spiritual elements that the century had amassed, acquired an unsuspected dynamic force and exalted all the individual and collective forces. The power which religion seems to have lost, this new faith inherited. It is a religion. It is the great hope in the "regeneration" of the men of France and even of humanity. It is essentially a moral revolution and through it a social revolution.

It is not, in truth, the financial deficit, however serious, nor the economic crisis, even more serious, nor the widespread popular misery, which was so profound and so lamentable; nor is it the loss of national prestige which was so patent, nor the refusal of the Notables and of the privileged members of the Clergy and of parlements to support the distressed monarchy with its wealth, which brought the French nation to revolution.

Undoubtedly it is all that, but above all, it is the heart leaping up to liberty. . . . It is a "mystique" which fills noble souls with a sacred fervor; it seems that they hover between Heaven and Earth. Thus, the "nation" of the Rights of Man will stand forth, proud and resolute before the people of the world. Despite everything that happened this is the ideal which will survive, which the soldier citizens of the Revolution will always hold before them, to sustain them and inspire them during their trials.

THE PARLEMENTS AND THE KING: CONSTITUTIONAL MONARCHY VERSUS ROYAL ABSOLUTISM[2]

The magistrates of the Parlement of Paris and those of the twelve provincial parlements endeavored during the entire eighteenth century to limit the absolutism of the king by invoking what they called "the constitution" of France. By the constitution they meant the totality of the laws, edicts, ordinances, judicial decisions which had come down through the long history of the monarchy and of which they claimed to be the guardians. Thus, there was long precedent for the revolt of the parlements in 1788. The first of the following passages is, perhaps, the most sweeping formulation of their claims. It was made by the Parlement of Rennes in Brittany in 1757. The second document is an excerpt from the speech of Louis XV at a Bed of Justice (lit de justice), *held in 1766, in which he vigorously reaffirmed the theory of royal absolutism.*

✓   ✓   ✓

I. The Remonstrance of the Parlement of Rennes, 1757

The functions which characterize parlement do not consist in judging a few trials of private individuals. . . . One isolated section of the rights of the magistrate can-

---

[2] The two excerpts given here are translated from the French: (I), from Archives départementales d'Ille-et-Vilaine (A.P.), B. 72. *Remontrances du 12 août, 1757;* (II), from J. Flammermont et M. Tourneux (eds.), *Remontrances du Parlement de Paris* (Paris, 1895), II, pp. 556-558.

not be regarded as the equivalent of that full authority of the body of magistrates which constitutes the essential rights and functions of parlement. To judge the equity and usefulness of new laws, the interest of the state and the public, to maintain order and peace in the kingdom, to exercise sovereign jurisdiction and general policy control over all matters, all things, all persons, such are the rights and the basic functions, exclusive and unique, of parlement. Decisions in the trials of individuals is included within them only in consequence of and in the same way that a part is included in the whole.

II. Louis XV Rebukes the Parlements, 1766

What has taken place in my parlements of Pau and Rennes has nothing to do with my other parlements; I have acted in regard to these two courts as befits my authority and I do not have to account for it to anyone.

I would not have any other answer to give to so many remonstrances that have been made to me on that score, if their number, the impropriety of their style, the temerity of the most erroneous principles, and the affectation of the new terms in which they are couched, did not exhibit the noxious results of this system of unity [*their claim to be a single organic body rather than thirteen distinct courts*], which I have already proscribed and which they would like to establish in principle while at the same time daring to put it into practice.

I will not suffer any association to be formed in my realm which would make the natural bond of like duties and common obligations degenerate into a confederation of resistance, nor will I suffer that an imaginary corporative body creep into the monarchy that could only disturb the concord within it. The magistracy in no way constitutes a corporative body or an order separate from the three estates of the kingdom; magistrates are my officers, charged with performing for me a duty truly royal, that of dispensing justice to my subjects. . . . I know the importance of their services: thus it is but an illusion which tends only to shatter confidence by false alarms to pretend that there is a plan to destroy the magistracy and to suggest that it has enemies in royal circles. Its sole and its real enemies are those in its midst who inspire it to speak a language opposed to its principles; who instigate it to say that all parlements make up but a sole and single body . . . ; that this body is the essence of the monarchy and that it serves the monarchy as a base; that it is the protector and the basic depository of its liberty, its interests, and its rights . . . ; that it is responsible for all parts of the public good, not only to the king, but to the nation; that it is judge between the king and his people . . . ; that the parlements share with the sovereign power the right of establishing the laws; that they can on occasion and by their sole efforts nullify a registered law and rightly consider it nonexistent. . . . To attempt to institute such pernicious innovations is, in principle, to do injury to the magistracy, to belie its foundation, to betray its interests, and to misconceive the true, fundamental laws of the state; as though one might be allowed to forget that it is in my being alone that the sovereign power resides . . . ; that it is from me alone that my courts derive their existence and their authority; that the plenitude of this authority, which they exercise only in my name, always rests with me . . . ; that it is to me alone that the legislative power appertains without any dependence and without any division [*of authority*]; that it is by my authority alone that the officers of my courts carry on their work, not the making of law, but registering it, publishing it, and giving force to it; and that they are allowed to make remonstrances to me, as is the duty of good and useful councillors; that the whole public order emanates from me and that the rights and interests of the nation which they dare to distinguish from the monarch are necessarily united with mine and rest only in my hands.

— Reading No. 3 —

TURGOT'S EDICTS ABOLISHING THE CORVÉE AND THE GUILDS[3]

The most determined and comprehensive attempt made during the last years of the Ancien Regime *to eradicate old abuses and provide a sound foundation for national economy was made by the experienced administrator and* philosophe, *Jacques Turgot. Supported briefly by Louis XVI, he proposed a program of reforms which, unfortunately, was opposed when it was presented, and sabotaged during its brief period of acceptance by several groups that had a vested interest in maintaining the status quo. The first reading is an excerpt from the preamble accompanying his edict to do away with the royal corvée; the second gives his reasons for abolishing the craft guilds.*

✓   ✓   ✓

I. Turgot's Edict on the Corvée (1776)

. . . We have noted with pain that, with the exception of a small number of provinces, works of this kind have been executed, for the most part, by means of corvées required of our subjects, and even from the poorest part, while they have been paid no wages for the time they were so employed. . . .

---

[3] Both of these selections come from the Six Projects of Edicts that Turgot proposed and the Royal Council adopted in 1776. They are translated by R. P. Shepherd, in his *Turgot and the Six Edicts* (New York, 1903), pp. 147-148, 151-152 for (I), and pp. 186-187 for (II). Reprinted by permission of the Columbia University Press.

To draft the cultivator forcibly to these labors is always to do him a real wrong, even when he is paid for his day's work. One would seek in vain to select, for demanding forced labor, a time when the peasants were unoccupied; the work of cultivation is so diversified and so incessant that no time is without its employment. . . . The most attentive administrators cannot know all these variations. . . . Error on the part of the administrator may cause to the cultivators a loss of days for which no salary could repay them.

To take the time of the laborer, even for pay, is equivalent to a tax. To take this time without paying for it is a double tax; and that tax is out of all proportion when it falls on a simple day-laborer who has nothing for his subsistence but the labor of his hands.

The man who works under compulsion and without recompense works idly and without interest; he does, at the same time, less work, and his work is poorly done. The peasants (corvoyeurs), obliged to travel frequently ten miles or more to report to the foreman, and as much more to return to their homes, lose a great part of the time demanded from them, without any labor return for it. The multiplied complaints, the embarrassment of tracing out the work, of distributing it, of executing it with a lot of men gathered haphazard, most of them as devoid of intelligence as they are of initiative, consume a further part of the remaining time. In this way the work which is done costs the people and the state, in day's labor of men and vehicles, twice and often three times what it would cost if done for a money consideration. . . .

The weight of that charge does not fall, nor can it ever fall, anywhere else than upon the poorest part of our subjects, upon those who have no property other than their hands and their industry, upon the peasants and on the farmers. The landowners, almost all of whom are *privilégiés*, being exempt, contribute but very little.

Nevertheless it is to the landowners that the public roads are useful, by the value which increased channels of communication give to the products of their lands. It is not the actual farmers nor the day-laborers who work for them that are profited. The successors of the present farmers will pay to the proprietors that increase of value in increase of rents. The class of day-laborers will gain, perhaps, some day an increase of wages proportionate to the increased price of commodities; . . . but the class of landowners alone will receive a prompt and immediate increase of wealth, and that new wealth will not be scattered among the people except in so far as the people will purchase it through increased labor.

It is then the class of proprietors of land which receives the fruit of the construction of roads; it is that class which ought alone to make the necessary advances, since they finally secure the benefits.

II. Turgot's Edict on the Guilds (1776)

We regard it as one of the first obligations of our justice, and as an act in every way worthy of our beneficence, to emancipate our subjects from all the restraints which have been laid upon that inalienable right of humanity. Wherefore, we will to abolish the arbitrary institutions which do not permit the indigent to live by their labor; . . . which stifle emulation and industry and make useless the talents of those whom circumstances exclude from admission into the guild; which deprive the state and art of all the advantages which foreigners might furnish; which retard the progress of the arts by the difficulties which inventors find multiplied by the guilds, . . . which, by means of the inordinate expenses artisans are compelled to incur in order to acquire the liberty of labor, by the exactions of all kinds they must endure, by the multiplied penalties for so-called offenses, by expense and extravagance of every sort, by the endless litigations which arise between the different associations, . . . surcharge industry with an enormous tax, grievous to the subjects and with no corresponding advantage to the state; which, in short, . . . become an instrument of monopoly and give rise to schemes whose effect is to increase beyond all natural proportion the price of commodities which are most necessary for the subsistence of the people. . . .

— Reading No. 4 —

THE REVOLT OF THE ARISTOCRACY [4]

In his endeavor to by-pass the opposition of the Parlement of Paris, which he realized would not register his reform edicts, Calonne summoned an Assembly of Notables (February, 1787). This body of 144 carefully selected representatives of the privileged orders (including wealthy financiers from the Third Estate) was cast for the role of a rubber-stamp congress. This it emphatically refused to accept. The first passage, which comes from Calonne's opening observations, is an eloquent denunciation of the abuses which deprived the monarchy of sorely-needed revenue. The following excerpts disclose the confident mood of the magistrates, the king's unwillingness to alienate them, and the fear that the pamphlet campaign inspired in the princes of the blood. The final selection is from Necker's preface to the decision of the Royal Council (December, 1788) to double the number of deputies from the Third Estate. It shows how without definitely committing himself or the government, Necker intimated that even on nonfinancial subjects the possibility existed that sooner or later the three orders might deliberate and vote by head. Because of divided opinion within the Council, he was unable to go beyond his am-

[4] These selections are all translated from vol. I (Paris, 1867), *Archives parlementaires, première série*, ed. by J. Mavidal and E. Laurent, in the following order: (I), pp. 194-195 and 201-207; (II A), pp. 279-284; (II B), pp. 487-489; (III), p. 492.

*biguous words, which were interpreted by each group
in a favorable sense.*

✔   ✔   ✔

I. Calonne before the Assembly of Notables

To continue to borrow would be to aggravate the evil
and to precipitate the ruin of the state.

To impose new taxes would be to overwhelm the people
whom the king wishes to relieve.

To borrow on future revenue, we have had too much
of that already. . . .

To economize is no doubt necessary . . . but economy
alone, however stringent it be, would be inadequate and
can be considered only as a secondary means.

What then remains to fill the frightening void, to en-
able us to attain the desired level? What remains that can
take the place of all that is lacking and to procure all
that would be necessary to put our finances in order?
The abuses. Yes, gentlemen, it is in the very abuses themselves that there lies a fund of wealth that the state has
the right to claim and that must serve to re-establish
financial order. It is in the ending of abuses that there
remains the sole means of providing for our needs. . . .

The abuses, the destruction of which today is the
point at issue for the public weal, are the most considerable, the most protected, and those which have the deepest roots and the most extensive branches. Such are the
abuses whose existence weighs upon the productive and
laboring class, abuses of pecuniary privileges, exceptions
to the common law, and so many unjust exemptions that
cannot relieve one section of taxpayers without aggravat-
ing the lot of others. . . .

If so many abuses . . . have up to now held fast
against public opinion which has condemned them and
the efforts of administrators who have attempted to
remedy them, it is because we wished by partial operations to perform what could not be done successfully
except by a general operation; it is because we believed
that we could cure disorder without destroying the germ,
it is because we had undertaken to improve the regime of
the state without correcting its discrepancies, without

restoring a principle of uniformity which alone can obviate difficulties of detail and revive the whole body of the monarchy. . . .

[*On the following day he made extensive comments on each of the reform edicts that he proposed*]: One cannot take a step in this vast realm without finding in it different laws, contrary usages, privileges, exemptions, compounding of taxes, rights and claims of every kind; and this general dissonance complicates administration, interrupts its course, impedes its functioning, and increases expenses and disorder everywhere. . . .

[*The salt tax*] is so disproportionate in its assessment that in one province people pay twenty times more than in another; so harsh in its collection that its name alone inspires terror; a tax which, striking as it does an item of prime necessity, weighs upon the poor almost as much as on the rich. . . . A tax, in short, which costs a fifth of its yield to collect and which by the tremendous opportunity that it offers for smuggling annually results in the condemnation of more than 500 heads of families to the chain gang or to prison, and is the occasion for more than 4,000 arrests. Such are the characteristic features of the *gabelle*.

II. Parlement and the Princes of the Blood (1788)

A. *The Remonstrance of the Parlement of Paris* (*April 11, 1788*): Sire, public liberty, attacked in its principle, despotism substituted for the law of the state, the magistracy, finally, reduced to being nothing more than the instrument of arbitrary power, such are the important and woeful matters which bring your parlement back to the foot of the throne. . . .

The meeting held by Your Majesty in his parlement the 19 of November last, that august session which, by bringing the truth closer to the throne, was to pave the way for ever strengthening liberty through reason, and trust through liberty, in the realm, would on the contrary only produce distrust with servitude; if an act of absolute power sufficed to efface the fundamental principles, historic proofs and positive laws upon which the rights of your subjects have rested for 1300 years.

It was not permitted your Parlement to maintain silence

upon so explicit an infringement upon the principles of the monarchy. . . .

The sole will of the king is not law in itself. . . . For this will to be binding it must legally be published; to be legally published, it must be freely verified; such Sire, is the French constitution; it was born with the monarchy. . . .

B. *The Memoir of the Princes of the Blood* (*December 12, 1788*): Sire, the state is in peril; Your Person is respected, but Sire, a revolution is taking place in the principles of government. It is caused by the ferment of minds. Institutions reputed sacred and under which this monarchy has prospered for so many centuries are laid open to criticism, even decried as unjust. . . .

Everything proclaims and proves the existence of a system of deliberate insubordination and contempt for the laws of the state. . . .

Such is the unfortunate advance of this effervescence that opinions which at one time would have appeared most reprehensible, today appear reasonable and just. What today makes respectable people indignant in a little while will be accepted as right and legitimate. Who can say at what point the rashness of these opinions will stop? The rights of the throne have been questioned; public opinion is divided on the question of the rights of the two orders of the state; soon the rights of property will be attacked; the inequality of fortunes will be offered as a matter for reform; already, the abolition of feudal rights has been proposed, on the ground that feudalism is a system of oppression, a survival of barbarism.

Let the Third Estate stop attacking the rights of the two first orders; rights no less old than the monarchy itself should be as inalterable as its constitution; let it limit itself to requesting the reduction of taxes with which it is perhaps overloaded; then, the first two orders, recognizing in the third [*estate*] citizens who are dear to them, will be able, by the generosity of their sentiment, renounce those prerogatives which pertain to pecuniary interest and agree to bear in the most perfect equality the burden of public taxation.

III. Necker's Preface to the *Result of the Council* (December, 1788)

By its personal wealth and its loans to the government the Third Estate is linked with public finance. Knowledge and enlightenment have become a common heritage. Prejudices are weakened. Since the old deliberation by orders could not be changed except through the agreement of the three orders and with the approval of the king, the number of deputies of the Third Estate is for the present only a way of gathering information which can be useful to the welfare of the state. One cannot deny that this variety of knowledge belongs particularly to the order of the Third Estate, since there are a multitude of public matters on which it alone is instructed, such as: the transaction of internal and foreign commerce, the state of manufactures, methods most suitable for encouraging them, public credit, interest rates and circulation of money, the abuses of tax collecting, that of privileges, and so many others of which it alone has had experience. . . . The desire of the Third Estate, when it is unanimous, when it conforms to the principles of justice, always will call itself the national will. Time will sanction it, the approval of Europe will encourage it, and the sovereign can only regulate through his justice or anticipate through his wisdom what circumstances and opinions in themselves must bring about.

— Reading No. 5 —

PAMPHLETS AND CAHIERS[5]

[5] The excerpts from (I) *What Is the Third Estate?* come from the translation by J. H. Stewart, in *A Documentary Survey of the French Revolution* (New York, 1951), pp. 42, 44, 45, 52. The cahiers (II) are translated from the text as quoted in A. Soboul, *1789, "l'An Un de la Liberté,"* 2nd ed. (Paris, 1950), pp. 80-82; 85-86, respectively. The Stewart translation is reprinted by permission of The Macmillan Company.

Of the thousand or more pamphlets that were printed and circulated from 1788 to 1789, that of the Abbé Sieyès, What Is the Third Estate? *from which excerpts are given, was easily the most influential. The following documents are excerpted from two primary cahiers from the province of Languedoc, the cahier of the Third Estate of a small community of fewer than 500 inhabitants, Valleraugue in the Cévennes, and the cahier of the Third Estate of the town of Beaucaire, with a population of two thousand.*

✓   ✓   ✓

I. *What Is the Third Estate?*

The plan of this pamphlet is very simple. We have three questions to ask:

1st. What is the third estate? Everything.

2nd. What has it been heretofore in the political order? Nothing.

3rd. What does it demand? To become something therein.

We shall see if the answers are correct. Then we shall examine the measures that have been tried and those which must be taken in order that the third estate may in fact become *something.* Thus we shall state:

4th. What the ministers have *attempted,* and what the privileged classes themselves *propose* in its favor.

5th. What *ought* to have been done.

6th. Finally, what *remains* to be done in order that the third estate may take its rightful place. . . .

Who, then, would dare to say that the third estate has not within itself all that is necessary to constitute a complete nation? If the privileged order were abolished, the nation would be not something less but something more. Thus, what is the third estate? Everything; but an everything shackled and oppressed. What would it be without the privileged order? Everything; but an everything free and flourishing. Nothing can progress without it; everything would proceed infinitely better without the others. . . .

Let us examine its position in the Estates General.

Who have been its so-called representatives? The ennobled or those privileged for a period of years. These false deputies have not even been always freely elected by the people. Sometimes in the Estates General, and almost always in the provincial Estates, the representation of the people has been regarded as a perquisite of certain posts or offices. . . .

Let us sum up: the third estate has not heretofore had real representatives in the Estates General. Thus its political rights are null. . . .

The true petitions of this order may be appreciated only through the authentic claims directed to the government by the large municipalities of the kingdom. What is indicated therein? That the people wishes to be *something,* and, in truth, the very least that is possible. It wishes to have real representatives in the Estates General, that is to say, deputies *drawn from its order,* who are competent to be interpreters of its will and defenders of its interests. But what will it avail it to be present at the Estates General if the predominating interest there is contrary to its own! Its presence would only consecrate the oppression of which it would be the eternal victim. Thus, it is indeed certain that it cannot come to vote at the Estates General unless it is to have in that body *an influence at least equal to that of the privileged classes;* and it demands a number of representatives equal to that of the first two orders together. Finally, this equality of representation would become completely illusory if every chamber voted separately. The third estate demands, then, that votes be taken *by head and not by order*. This is the essence of those claims so alarming to the privileged classes, because they believed that thereby the reform of abuses would become inevitable. . . .

In such a state of affairs, what must the third estate do if it wishes to gain possession of its political rights in a manner beneficial to the nation? There are two ways of attaining this objective. In following the first, the third estate must assemble apart: it will not meet with the nobility and the clergy at all; it will not remain with them, either by *order* or by *head*. I pray that they will keep in mind the enormous difference between the assembly of the third estate and that of the other two orders. The first represents 25,000,000 men, and deliberates concerning the interests of the nation. The two others, were they to unite, have the powers of only about 200,000 individuals, and think only of their privileges. The third estate alone, they say, cannot constitute the *Estates General*. Well! So much the better! it will form a *National Assembly*. . . .

II. Two Primary Cahiers

A. *Cahier of the Community of Valleraugue:* The King is most humbly beseeched:

In the first place: To accord to this province of Languedoc the right to assemble and form its special estates in the way that it judges most suitable, by admitting to this assembly members of the Third Estate at least equal in number to that of the two other orders combined.

2. To order that all citizens, without distinction of orders be called upon to contribute to all expenses, present or future, in proportion to their incomes and abilities, of whatever nature they be.

3. To oblige the tithe-owners to grant to the curés a portion really and truly adequate, that is to say, suitable, sufficient and capable of supporting them in making a living in a decent fashion and of permitting them to exercise their charity toward the poor.

4. To be willing to reform the civil and criminal codes, to abridge and simplify the judicial forms, to decrease the costs of justice, the length of the trials, and the number of legal agents, to bring the sovereign courts of justice closer in such a way so that the poor farmer no longer will be obliged to seek justice fifty leagues away from his home; to abolish the courts of exception, and if possible the venality of offices.

5. To abrogate also all the laws and the regulations which harm agriculture . . . and to modify, above all, those laws which forbid the transfer of wealth pertaining to dowry rights [*and*] the sale of the estates of minors. . . .

6. To suppress the *gabelle* as destructive to agriculture and to replace this tax, if there be need, by a tax levied in money in conformity with the opinion of Monsieur [*king's brother*], as contained in the minutes of the first Assembly of Notables.

7. To secure the individual liberty of citizens and not

to punish anyone without a hearing and without observing the forms prescribed by the ordinances.

8. To order that in the future the community as a whole bear the expenses for its militiamen.

9. To arrest the inroads of celibacy by according advantages and benefits upon married people, while increasing by one quarter the rate of the personal tax of bachelors.

10. Finally, to bear in mind that the *pays* of the Hautes-Cévennes is unable to stand an increase in taxes because, on the one hand, its soil, by its very location, depreciates in value every day and grows more and more sour and unyielding; and on the other hand, the price of mulberry leaves, the sole source of income of this little area, which, only thirty years ago, brought two measures of wheat, today buys only one and a quarter.

Done and drawn up in two originals, the day and year above, by the citizens making up the said assembly, and those who were able to sign, having signed.

B. *The Cahier of the Third Estate of Beaucaire:*

1. The deputies of the commons of this city will be instructed to present their wishes for the suppression of the existing Estates of the province and the drawing up of a new constitution with free and equal representation. And to this end a general assembly of the three orders will be requested. The deputies to protest against the regime of the said estates and to authorize the deputies of the diocese in Paris to beseech with all their might the execution of the present article.

2. The deputies to the Estates General will direct all their efforts toward making the voting be by head and not by order.

3. A declaration of the rights of man and of the citizen.

4. Liberty of the press and the security of publications, and in this respect the public trust may not be violated in any place and in any case.

5. The abolition of *lettres de cachet* and every arbitrary act prejudicial to the liberty of the citizen.

6. Proportional equality of contributions upon persons and goods without distinction.

7. A commission will be nominated for the reform of criminal laws.

8. A second commission for the reform of civil laws.

12. The suppression of toils . . . and other rights of this nature by means of just and reasonable indemnities in favor of the owners.

13. To request that in the re-assessment of taxes all those harmful to commerce and industry be done away with.

14. Freedom of perpetual lease-holders to free themselves from rights which weigh heavily upon them by means of a payment of real, effective and proportional compensation to their lords.

16. That different positions in the military and naval forces and in the high magistracy be made accessible to all members of the Third Estate.

17. The freedom of persons of the Third Estate to carry arms with suitable restrictions.

— Reading No. 6 —

THE JUNE DAYS OF 1789[6]

The deliberate policy of the deputies of the Third Estate to refrain from verifying their credentials separately reached a dramatic climax on June 17. On that day they took a revolutionary step by formally conferring upon themselves the title of National Assembly. They reaffirmed their disobedience of Louis XVI three days

[6] The translations from the French are all from F. M. Anderson, *Constitutions and Documents Illustrative of the History of France, 1789-1901* (New York, 1904), pp. 1-2; 3-4; and 10-11.

later by swearing the Tennis Court Oath and again on
June 23 by refusing to adjourn when ordered to do so.

✓   ✓   ✓

I. The Creation of the National Assembly
(June 17, 1789)

The Assembly, deliberating after the verification of
the powers, recognizes that this assembly is already
composed of the representatives sent directly by at least
ninety-six per cent of the nation.

Such a body of deputies cannot remain inactive owing
to the absence of the deputies of some bailliages and
some classes of citizens; for the absentees, who have been
summoned, cannot prevent those present from exercising
the full extent of their rights, especially when the exercise
of these rights is an imperious and pressing duty.

Furthermore, since it belongs only to the verified representatives to participate in the formation of the national opinion, and since all the verified representatives
ought to be in this assembly, it is still more indispensable
to conclude that the interpretation and presentation of
the general will of the nation belong to it, and belong to
it alone, and that there cannot exist between the throne
and this assembly any veto, any negative power.—The
Assembly declares then that the common task of the national restoration can and ought to be commenced without delay by the deputies present and that they ought
to pursue it without interruption as well as without
hindrance.—The denomination of NATIONAL AS-
SEMBLY is the only one which is suitable for the
Assembly in the present condition of things; because the
members who compose it are the only representatives
lawfully and publicly known and verified; because they are
sent directly by almost the totality of the nation; because,
lastly, the representation being one and indivisible, none
of the deputies, in whatever class or order he may be
chosen, has the right to exercise his functions apart from
the present assembly. . . . The National Assembly orders
that the motives of the present decision be immediately
drawn up in order to be presented to the King and the
nation.

II. The Tennis Court Oath (June 20, 1789)

The National Assembly, considering that it has been summoned to determine the Constitution of the kingdom, to effect the regeneration of public order, to maintain the true principles of the monarchy; that nothing can prevent it from continuing its deliberations in whatever place it may be forced to establish itself, and lastly, that wherever its members meet together, there is the National Assembly.

Decrees that all the members of this Assembly shall immediately take a solemn oath never to separate, and to reassemble wherever circumstances shall require, until the Constitution of the kingdom shall be established and consolidated upon firm foundation; and that, the said oath being taken, all the members and each of them individually shall ratify by their signatures this steadfast resolution.

III. Proceedings of June 23

A. *Declaration of Louis XVI concerning the Estates General:* The King wishes that the ancient distinction of the three Orders of the State be preserved in its entirety, as essentially linked to the constitution of his Kingdom; that the deputies, freely elected by each of the three Orders, forming three chambers, deliberating by Order . . . can alone be considered as forming the body of the representatives of the Nation. As a result, the King has declared null the resolutions passed by the deputies of the Order of the Third Estate, the 17th of this month, as well as those which have followed them, as illegal and unconstitutional. . . .

B. *Declaration of the King's Intentions:* [*After he had stated his intentions, the King declared:*] *I order you, gentlemen, to separate immediately, and to go tomorrow morning, each to the chamber allotted to your Order; in order to take up again your sessions. I order therefore the Grand Master of Ceremonies, to have the halls prepared.*

C. *Decree of the Assembly:* The National Assembly de-

clares that the person of each of the deputies is inviolable;
that all individuals, all corporations, tribunal, court or
commission that shall dare during or after the present
session, to pursue, to seek for, to arrest or have arrested,
detain or have detained, a deputy, by reason of any propo-
sitions, advice, opinions, or discourse made by him in the
States-General; as well as all persons who shall lend their
aid to any of the said attempts by whomsoever they may
be ordered, are infamous and traitors to the Nation and
guilty of capital crime. The National Assembly decrees
that, in the aforesaid cases, it will take all the necessary
measures to have sought out, pursued and punished those
who may be its authors, instigators, or executors.

— Reading No. 7 —

FRANCE, 1789-1791 [7]

*With the press virtually free in the first years of the
Revolution, despite regulating acts by the public authorities, journalists did not hesitate to color the news or make
comments, as the excerpts concerning the king's trip to
Paris after the fall of the Bastille, the session of August
4, and the October days vividly indicate. In view of the*

[7] The following readings, translated from the French, are respectively: (I A), from *Journal politique national*, No. 8;
(I B), from Loustalot's *Révolutions de Paris*, No. 4;
(I C), from F. M. Anderson, *op. cit.*, pp. 58-60; (I D),
from Camille Desmoulins' *Révolution de France et de
Brabant*, No. 1. (II A) is taken from Marquis du Fer-
rières, *Mémoires*, 2 vols. (Paris, 1823), I, p. 170; (II B)
is from *Le Point du Jour*, No. 168; and (II C) from
B. S. Buchez and P. C. Roux, *Histoire parlementaire de la
révolution française*, 40 vols. (Paris, 1834-1838), IX,
p. 469.

importance of the Declaration of Rights of Man and Citizen, the text is given in its entirety. The hopeful mood of the Parisians in 1790 is illustrated by the excerpt concerning their preparations to celebrate the first anniversary of the capture of the Bastille, while the two brief passages from Robespierre's speeches in the assembly are representative of democratic criticism of the Constitution of 1791.

✓   ✓   ✓

I. The End of the Ancien Regime

A. *A Royalist Journalist Comments on the King's Acceptance of the July 14 Revolution:* His Majesty, seeing that it would be necessary to drown the insurrection in pools of blood, preferred to recognize it by dint of his clemency. He appeared without preliminary ceremonies before the States General which for the first time he called the National Assembly. He confirmed the dismissal of the army camped around Paris, approved the establishment of the bourgeois militia, handed a letter for the recall of Necker to the president of the assembly, authorized eighty deputies to be sent to Paris to bring the tidings of his generosity and, by his silence, ignored the defection of the French Guard and the murder of his officers.

But, if Paris frightened Versailles, no less did Versailles terrify Paris. The capital, which could not believe in so much clemency on the part of the King, barricaded its streets and was covered with armed men who seemed to have sprung from the earth. . . . The national cockade was hoisted everywhere; it was white, blue, and red. These colors decorated everything, sanctioned everything, justified everything.

. . . These successes led on to others and the appetite for power could not be appeased. The City Hall and the bourgeoisie of Paris, not content with the sacrifices which His Majesty had made to keep the public peace, and in the first drunken throes of sovereignty, demanded that His Majesty come to the capital to show it a king without an army, without ministers, without a council, and since it must be said, a king stripped [*of his powers*]: His

Majesty, with an instinct which we would call genius, if we did not fear to denigrate the goodness of his heart, confounded the evil-minded and all those who had counted upon his taking an extreme stand or at least upon a little resistance: he announced that he would go to Paris. . . .

It was on the 17th of June that the Third Estate declared itself the National Assembly and it was on the 17th of the following month that the King confirmed the new order of things by going to Paris. Versailles will never forget that day and that departure: the King's former servants could not, without shedding tears, watch the French monarch, whose very name was invested with thoughts of love and authority, proceed without ceremony and without defence, in the midst of an armed populace, toward a capital in delirium, in order to sanction an insurrection.

B. *The Parisians Learn of the August 4 Decrees:* That night [August 5] several people who had been present at the meeting of the National Assembly held the night before, announced the news that the Constitution had been drawn up on all points concerning feudalism and upon others equally essential. A short time later, a printed account of the substance of the national debate was distributed.

A frenzy of joy immediately burst forth in all hearts; everyone congratulated one another; they enthusiastically called our deputies Fathers of the Country. It seemed as though a new day were about to dawn in France. In short, although they expected all the benefits of wisdom on the part of the National Assembly, it seemed that they had just received an unhoped-for blessing from it.

Groups formed on all the main streets. Near all the bridges they waited for passersby, so to speak, to apprize them of what, perhaps, they would not have learned until the morrow. They were happy to share their joy, to spread it. Fraternity, sweet fraternity, reigned everywhere. It was especially when people chanced to meet any French Guards that the demonstrations of joy were most enthusiastic. Some Guardsmen were seen embracing bourgeois who clasped them in their arms. Yes, there are moments in the lives of peoples as in those of men, which make them forget the years of grief and calamity.

C. *The Declaration of Rights of Man and Citizen:* The representatives of the French people, organized in National Assembly, considering that ignorance, forgetfulness or contempt of the rights of man are the sole causes of the public miseries and of the corruption of governments, have resolved to set forth in a solemn declaration the natural, inalienable, and sacred rights of man, in order that this declaration, being ever present to all the members of the social body, may unceasingly remind them of their rights and their duties: in order that the acts of the legislative power and those of the executive power may be each moment compared with the aim of every political institution and thereby may be more respected; and in order that the demands of the citizens, grounded henceforth upon simple and incontestable principles, may always take the direction of maintaining the constitution and the welfare of all.

In consequence, the National Assembly recognizes and declares, in the presence and under the auspices of the Supreme Being, the following rights of man and citizen.

1. Men are born and remain free and equal in rights. Social distinctions can be based only upon public utility.

2. The aim of every political association is the preservation of the natural and imprescriptible rights of man. These rights are liberty, property, security, and resistance to oppression.

3. The source of all sovereignty is essentially in the nation; no body, no individual can exercise authority that does not proceed from it in plain terms.

4. Liberty consists in the power to do anything that does not injure others; accordingly, the exercise of the natural rights of each man has for its only limits those that secure to the other members of society the enjoyment of these same rights. These limits can be determined only by law.

5. The law has the right to forbid only such actions as are injurious to society. Nothing can be forbidden that is not interdicted by the law and no one can be constrained to do that which it does not order.

6. Law is the expression of the general will. All citizens have the right to take part personally or by their representatives in its formation. It must be the same for all, whether it protects or punishes. All citizens being equal in its eyes are equally eligible to all public dignities, places, and employments, according to their capacities, and without other distinction than that of their virtues and their talents.

7. No man can be accused, arrested, or detained except in the cases determined by the law and according to the forms that it has prescribed. Those who procure, expedite, execute, or cause to be executed arbitrary orders ought to be punished; but every citizen summoned or seized in virtue of the law ought to render instant obedience; he makes himself guilty by resistance.

8. The law ought to establish only penalties that are strictly and obviously necessary and no one can be punished except in virtue of a law established and promulgated prior to the offence and legally applied.

9. Every man being presumed innocent until he has been pronounced guilty, if it is thought indispensable to arrest him, all severity that may not be necessary to secure his person ought to be strictly suppressed by law.

10. No one ought to be disturbed on account of his opinions, even religious, provided their manifestation does not derange the public order established by law.

11. The free communication of ideas and opinions is one of the most precious of the rights of man; every citizen then can freely speak, write, and print, subject to responsibility for the abuse of this freedom in the cases determined by law.

12. The guarantee of the rights of man and citizen requires a public force; this force then is instituted for the advantage of all and not for the personal benefit of those to whom it is entrusted.

13. For the maintenance of the public force and for the expenses of administration the general tax is indispensable; it ought to be equally apportioned among all the citizens according to their means.

14. All the citizens have the right to ascertain, by themselves or by their representatives, the necessity of the public tax, to consent to it freely, to follow the em-

ployment of it, and to determine the quota, the assessment, the collection, and the duration of it.

15. Society has the right to call for an account from every public agent of its administration.

16. Any society in which the guarantee of the rights is not secured or the separation of powers not determined has no constitution at all.

17. Property being a sacred and inviolable right, no one can be deprived of it unless a legally established public necessity evidently demands it, under the condition of a just and prior indemnity.

D. *Rejoicing Over the October Days: Consummatum est,* all is ended. The King is in the Louvre. The National Assembly is at the Tuileries. Channels of traffic are cleared, the Halles are bursting with sacks of grain, the national coffers are filled, mills are turning, traitors are fleeing, the clergy is humbled, the aristocracy is expiring, the schemes of the Mouniers and Lallys [*Lally-Tollendal, one of the moderate deputies*] are foiled, the provinces are cooperating and do not want to be separated [*from the capital*]. The Constitution is signed. Paris has escaped bankruptcy, it has escaped famine, it has escaped the massacre which threatened it. Paris is going to be the queen of cities and the splendor of the capital will correspond to the greatness and the majesty of the French state. . . .

We can say to the National Assembly, at present you have no more enemies, no more opponents, no more veto to fear. All that remains is for you to govern France, to make it happy and to give it such laws that by your example all peoples will be eager to transplant them and to make them flourish in their own lands.

II. Problems of Regenerated France

A. *The Fête de la Fédération, July 14, 1790:* Twelve thousand workers toiled ceaselessly to get the Champ-de-Mars ready. Notwithstanding the great energy devoted to the task, they made slow progress. There was fear that it could not be finished by July 14th. . . . In this embarrassing state of affairs, in the name of the *Patrie,* the districts invite good citizens to join the workers. This civic call electrifies all hearts. Women share the enthusiasm and spread it. One sees seminary students, schoolboys, mendicant sisters, Carthusian monks grown old in solitude, leaving their cloisters and running to the Champde-Mars, spade on back, carrying banners decorated with patriotic emblems. There, all citizens, miscellaneous, mingled, form an immense and mobile workshop where each section presents a varied group . . . the Capuchin monk drags a dray with the Chevalier de Saint-Louis, the stevedore with a dandy from the Palais Royal, a sturdy fishwife pushes the wheelbarrow filled by an elegant lady with the vapours; the well-to-do, the destitute, the well-dressed, those in tatters, the aged, children, actors . . . clerks, working and resting together, participants and onlookers, offer to the astonished eye a scene full of life and movement. Taverns and shops on wheels add to the charm and gaiety of this vast and delightful tableau; songs, cries of joy, the sound of drums, spades, wheelbarrows, the voices of workers who shout to each other, who encourage one another.

B. *Robespierre Defends the Political Rights of Jews* (*1789*): How could one, M. Robespierre exclaimed, accuse the Jews of persecutions of which they themselves have been the victims in different countries? On the contrary, those are national crimes which we should expiate by restoring to them the imprescriptible rights of man of which no human power could deprive them. Vices are still ascribed to them; and prejudice, sectarian spirit, and calculation exaggerates these vices. But on whom can we blame them, if not on our own injustice? After having excluded them from all honors, even the right to public esteem, have we not left them only opportunity for lucrative speculations? Restore them to happiness, to the *Patrie,* to virtue by giving back to them the dignity of men and of citizens. Let us remember that it can never be politic, whatever one may say, to condemn a large group of men living in our midst to degradation and oppression. How could the interests of society be grounded upon the violation of the eternal principles of justice and reason which are the very basis of all human society?

C. *Robespierre's Defense of the Political Rights of Colored Men in the Colonies (1791):* . . . But what then, especially in colonies, are the civil rights left to men [*i.e., colored*] without political rights? What is a man deprived of the rights of an active citizen in colonies under the domination of whites? He is a man who cannot take part in any way in political deliberations, who cannot influence, either directly or indirectly, the most moving, the most sacred interests of society of which he is a member. He is a man who is governed by magistrates whose selection he cannot determine in any way; by laws, by regulations, by administrative acts weighing heavily upon him, without having exercised that right which belongs to all citizens of sharing in social agreements which pertain to his own particular interests. He is a degraded being whose fate is left to caprice, to passions, to the interests of a higher caste.

— Reading No. 8 —

THE FIRST RESPONSES FROM ABROAD [8]

[8] Readings (I A, B) come from the translations in G. P. Gooch, *Germany and the French Revolution* (London, 1920), pp. 41, 43, and 47, respectively. These are reprinted by permission of Longmans, Green, and Company. (I C) is translated from *Briefe von und an Friedrich von Gentz,* ed. by F. C. Wittichen (Munich, 1909), I, pp. 178-179. (II A) is cited from *Works of Edmund Burke* (London, 1872-1873), II, pp. 306-309; (II B), from Thomas Paine, *The Rights of Man* (London, 1791), pp. 43-52. The two brief excerpts which make up (III A) are (1), from A. A. Lipscomb and A. E. Bergh (eds.), *The Writings of Thomas Jefferson* (Washington, 1905), VII, pp. 253-254, and (2), *Massachusetts Centinel* (September 23, 1789); the four passages that constitute

Contemporaries followed French developments closely in Europe and the United States. Newspapers, letters, and oral accounts from returning travellers to France kept them abreast of what was happening, although those reports were frequently fragmentary and almost always colored by the feelings of the narrators. The first group of readings shows the enthusiastic response of German men of letters, while the third set of excerpts illustrates the range of opinion in the United States. The two lengthy excerpts which constitute the second group of selections come from Burke and Paine, respectively.

✓   ✓   ✓

I. The German Intellectuals

A. *J. H. Campe, the Brunswick Pedagogue, Reports from Paris:* Is it really true [*August 4, 1789*] that I am in Paris? That the new Greeks and Romans whom I see around me were only a few weeks ago Frenchmen? That the great and wonderful drama which has been and is being performed is not a dream? I left home with the hope that I should arrive in time to attend the funeral of French despotism; and my hope is being fulfilled. The mortal blow has been struck at the heart of the dragon, and I found the hydra lying in its own blood; but there is still life in its hundred heads, and it still writhes in the dust, unwilling to yield up its black spirit. But die it will and must, and I shall not return till I see it entombed. [*And in his letter of August 26*]: The more I see of it the more profoundly convinced am I that the French Revolution is the greatest wholesale blessing vouchsafed by Providence to mankind since Luther; and all men, white and black, yellow and brown, ought to cry, Thank God for it.

(III B) are from (1) *Massachusetts Centinel* (September 19, 1789), (2) *Columbian Centinel* (June 4, 1791), (3) *New York Journal and Patriotic Register* (April 1, 1790 and November 29, 1790), and (4) *New York Daily Advertiser* (March 21, 1791). The four abridged passages cited in (III C) come from C. D. Hazen, *Contemporary American Opinion of the French Revolution* (Baltimore, 1897), pp. 81, 152-153, 143-144, and 159, respectively.

B. *Johann von Müller, the Historian, August 6, 1789:*
What a spectacle it is! I hope that many a Sultan in the
Empire will have a salutary shiver, and many an oli-
garchy learn that things cannot be pushed too far. I am
aware of the excesses; but they are not too great a price
to pay for a free constitution. Can there be any question
that a clearing storm, even when it works some havoc, is
better than the plague? [*And to his brother, same day*]:
July 14 is the best day since the fall of the Roman Empire.

C. *Friedrich von Gentz Writing in 1791:* I should regard
the failure of this Revolution as one of the cruelest misfortunes that ever befell mankind. The Revolution is the
first practical triumph of philosophy, the first example
of a form of government based on definite principles and
embodying a consistent system of ideas. It is our hope
and solace for so many hoary evils under which mankind
is sighing. If it failed, all these evils would return ten
times more incurable. . . . It would be felt that men
could be happy only as slaves, and every tyrant, great or
small, would use this confession to revenge himself for
the fright that the awakening of the French nation had
given him. In regard to the news from France, two considerations must be kept in mind—first, the incredible
stupidity and untrustworthiness of our miserable press,
and second, the fact that we get most of it from enemies of
the Revolution. Those who furnish us our information
are almost always compelled by fear of their governments to suppress any favorable features. . . . And I
assure you that all . . . complaints and sarcasms do not
in the least prevent me from seeing that the Assembly is
still acting wisely, that the excesses and disorders are
much exaggerated, that the future is more hopeful than
its enemies allow, and that if no unforeseen obstacles
arise, a happy end will crown the greatest work of history.

II. The Great Debate: Burke and Paine

A. Burke's *Reflections on the Revolution in France*
(*1790*): You will observe, that from Magna Charta to
the Declaration of Right, it has been the uniform policy
of our constitution to claim and assert our liberties, as
an entailed inheritance derived to us from our forefathers

and to be transmitted to our posterity; as an estate specially belonging to the people of this kingdom, without any reference whatever to any other more general or prior right. By this means our constitution preserves a unity in so great a diversity of its parts. We have an inheritable crown; an inheritable peerage; and a House of Commons and a people inheriting privileges, franchises, and liberties, from a long line of ancestors.

This policy appears to me to be the result of profound reflection; of rather the happy effect of following nature, which is wisdom without reflection, and above it. A spirit of innovation is generally the result of a selfish temper, and confined views. People will not look forward to posterity, who never look backward to their ancestors. Besides, the people of England well know, that the idea of inheritance furnishes a sure principle of conservation, and a sure principle of transmission, without at all excluding a principle of improvement. It leaves acquisition free; but it secures what it acquires. Whatever advantages are obtained by a state proceeding on these maxims, are locked fast as in a sort of family settlement; grasped as in a kind of mortmain for ever. By a constitutional policy, working after the pattern of nature, we receive, we hold, we transmit our government and our privileges, in the same manner in which we enjoy and transmit our property and our lives. The institutions of policy, the goods of fortune, the gifts of providence, are handed down to us, and from us, in the same course and order. Our political system is placed in a just correspondence and symmetry with the order of the world, and with the mode of existence decreed to a permanent body composed of transitory parts; wherein by the disposition of a stupendous wisdom, moulding together the great mysterious incorporation of the human race, the whole, at one time, is never old, or middle-aged, or young, but, in a condition of unchangeable constancy, moves on through the varied tenor of perpetual decay, fall, renovation, and progression. Thus, by preserving the method of nature in the conduct of the state, in what we improve, we are never wholly new; in what we retain, we are never wholly obsolete. By adhering in this manner and on those principles to our forefathers, we are guided not by the superstition of antiquarians, but by the spirit of philosophic analogy. In this choice of inheritance we have given to our frame of polity the image of a relation in blood; binding up the constitution of our country with our dearest domestic ties; adopting our fundamental laws into the bosom of our family affections; keeping inseparable, and cherishing with the warmth of all their combined and mutually reflected charities, our state, our hearths, our sepulchres, and our altars.

Through the same plan of a conformity to nature in our artificial institutions, and by calling in the aid of her unerring and powerful instincts, to fortify the fallible and feeble contrivances of our reason, we have derived several other, and those no small benefits, from considering our liberties in the light of an inheritance. Always acting as if in the presence of canonized forefathers, the spirit of freedom, leading in itself to misrule and excess, is tempered with an awful gravity. This idea of a liberal descent inspires us with a sense of habitual native dignity, which prevents that upstart insolence almost inevitably adhering to and disgracing those who are the first acquirers of any distinction. By this means our liberty becomes a noble freedom. It carries an imposing and majestic aspect. It has a pedigree and illustrating ancestors. It has its bearings and its ensigns armorial. It has its gallery of portraits; its monumental inscriptions; its records, evidences, and titles. We procure reverence to our civil institutions on the principle upon which nature teaches us to revere individual men; on account of their age, and on account of those from whom they are descended. All your sophisters cannot produce anything better adapted to preserve a rational and manly freedom than the course that we have pursued, who have chosen our nature rather than our speculations, our breasts rather than our inventions, for the great conservatories and magazines of our rights and privileges.

You might, if you pleased, have profited by our example, and have given to your recovered freedom a correspondent dignity. Your privileges, though discontinued, were not lost to memory. Your constitution, it is true, whilst you were out of possession, suffered waste and dilapidation; but you possessed in some parts the walls, and, in all, the foundations, of a noble and venerable castle. You might have repaired those walls; you might have built on those old foundations. Your constitution was suspended before it was perfected; but you had the elements of a constitution very nearly as good as could be wished. In your old states you possessed that variety of parts corresponding with the various descriptions of which your community was happily composed; you had all that combination, and all that opposition of interests, you had that action and counteraction, which, in the natural and in the political world, from the reciprocal struggle of discordant powers, draws out the harmony of the universe. These opposed and conflicting interests, which you considered as so great a blemish in your old and in our present constitution, interpose a salutary check to all precipitate resolutions. They render deliberation a matter not of choice, but of necessity; they make all change a subject of compromise, which naturally begets moderation; they produce *temperaments* preventing the sore evil of harsh, crude, unqualified reformations, and rendering all the headlong exertions of arbitrary power, in the few or in the many, for ever impracticable. Through that diversity of members and interests, general liberty had as many securities as there were separate views in the several orders; whilst by pressing down the whole by the weight of a real monarchy, the separate parts would have been prevented from warping, and starting from their allotted places.

B. Thomas Paine, *The Rights of Man* (*1791*): Before anything can be reasoned upon to a conclusion, certain facts, principles, or data, to reason from, must be established, admitted, or denied. Mr. Burke, with his usual outrage, abuses the Declaration of the Rights of Man, published by the National Assembly of France as the basis on which the constitution of France is built. This he calls "paltry and blurred sheets of paper about the rights of man."—Does Mr. Burke mean to deny that man has any rights? If he does, then he must mean that there are no such things as rights anywhere, and that he has none himself, for who is there in the world but man? But if Mr.

Burke means to admit that man has rights, the question then will be: What are those rights, and how came man by them originally?

The error of those who reason by precedents drawn from antiquity, respecting the rights of man, is, that they do not go far enough into antiquity. They do not go the whole way. They stop in some of the intermediate stages of a hundred or a thousand years, and produce what was then done as a rule for the present day. This is no authority at all. If we travel still farther into antiquity, we shall find a direct contrary opinion and practice prevailing; and if antiquity is to be authority, a thousand such authorities may be produced, successively contradicting each other; but if we proceed on, we shall at last come out right; we shall come to the time when man came from the hand of his Maker. What was he then? Man. Man was his high and only title, and a higher cannot be given him.—But of titles I shall speak hereafter.

If any generation of men ever possessed the right of dictating the mode by which the world should be governed for ever, it was the first generation that existed; and if that generation did not do it, no succeeding generation can show any authority for doing it, nor set any up. The illuminating and divine principle of the equal rights of man (for it has its origin from the Maker of man) relates, not only to the living individuals, but to generations of men succeeding each other. Every generation is equal in rights to the generations which preceded it, by the same rule that every individual is born equal in rights with his contemporary.

Every history of the creation, and every traditionary account, whether from the lettered or unlettered world, however they may vary in their opinion or belief of certain particulars, all agree in establishing one point, the unity of man; by which I mean that man is all of one degree, and consequently that all men are born equal, and with equal natural rights, in the same manner as if posterity had been continued by creation instead of generation, the latter being only the mode by which the former is carried forward; and consequently, every child born into the world must be considered as deriving its existence from God. The world is as new to him as it was to the first man that existed, and his natural right in it is of the same kind.

Hitherto we have spoken only (and that but in part) of the natural rights of man. We have now to consider the civil rights of man, and to show how the one originates out of the other. Man did not enter into society to become worse than he was before, nor to have less rights than he had before, but to have those rights better secured. His natural rights are the foundation of all his civil rights. But in order to pursue this distinction with more precision, it will be necessary to mark the different qualities of natural and civil rights.

A few words will explain this. Natural rights are those which appertain to man in right of his existence. Of this kind are all the intellectual rights, or rights of the mind, and also all those rights of acting as an individual for his own comfort and happiness, which are not injurious to the natural rights of others. Civil rights are those which appertain to man in right of his being a member of society. Every civil right has for its foundation some natural right pre-existing in the individual, but to which his individual power is not in all cases, sufficiently competent. Of this kind are all those which relate to security and protection.

From this short review, it will be easy to distinguish between that class of natural rights which man retains after entering into society, and those which he throws into the common stock as a member of society.

The natural rights which he retains, are all those in which the power to execute is as perfect in the individual as the right itself. Among this class, as is before mentioned, are all the intellectual rights, or rights of the mind, consequently, religion is one of those rights. The natural rights which are not retained, are all those in which, though the right is perfect in the individual, the power to execute them is defective. They answer not his purpose. A man, by natural right, has a right to judge in his own cause, and so far as the right of the mind is concerned, he never surrenders it. But what availeth it him to judge, if he has not power to redress? He therefore deposits this right in the common stock of society, and

takes the arms of society, of which he is a part, in preference and in addition to his own. Society grants him nothing. Every man is a proprietor in society, and draws on
the capital as a matter of right. . . .

III. Echoes from the United States

A. *The Debt of the French Revolutionists to the Americans:*

1. Jefferson to Dr. Price (January 8, 1789):

Though celebrated writers of this and other countries
had already sketched good principles on the subject of
government, yet the American war seems first to have
awakened the thinking part of this nation in general from
the sleep of despotism in which they were sunk. The
officers who had been to America were worthy young
men, less shackled by habit and prejudice, and more ready
to assent to the dictates of common sense and common
right. They came back impressed with these. The press,
notwithstanding its shackles, began to disseminate them;
conversation, too, assumed new freedom; politics became
the theme of all societies, male and female, and a very
extensive and zealous party was formed, which may be
called the Patriotic party who, sensible of the abusive
government under which they lived, longed for occasions
of reforming it.

2. The *Massachusetts Centinel* (September 23, 1789):

The English foolishly assert that the French Patriots
have learnt the principles of liberty from them. They
forget that the first *Declaration of Rights* ever published
in France, was almost a copy of parts of the American
Constitution—and that the NOBLEMAN who has been
the principal animating cause of the French Revolution
—learnt during his residence in America, that here—and
only here—are the Rights of Man ascertained.

B. *Excerpts from the Press:*

1. The *Massachusetts Centinel* (September 19, 1789)
on the first news:

REVOLUTION IN FRANCE

BOSTON, SATURDAY, Sept. 19, 1789

By Capt. Barnard, arrived yesterday from London, we
have received papers to the 6th of August. . . . Those

papers are *filled* with accounts of one of the greatest REVOLUTIONS recorded in the annals of time—a Revolution which has restored to the Nation of France its long lost liberties—and taught its Monarch that the throne of Kings is never solid, unless founded on the LOVE AND FIDELITY of subjects.

2. The *Columbian Centinel* (June 4, 1791):

THE NATIONAL ASSEMBLY

Proceeds with steadiness and harmony in the great work of reorganizing the nation. . . . The great objects of the Constitution have been effected. . . . Some subordinate regulations were before the Assembly on the date of our papers; and they appeared to contemplate with pleasure the speedy arrival of the period which shall close their labors, and give to the French nation a legitimate Legislature.

We see nothing in the [*French*] papers of those riots, plots and stratagems which have so frequently been detailed in the London papers.

3. The *New York Journal and Patriotic Register* (1790):

The Nation, considering that a long succession of ages —that manner and opinion, altogether new, have entirely altered and changed its interests . . . has undertaken to form and establish a new one on the principles of perfect freedom. This is the most important event which has happened in the old World for many ages [*from the issue of April 1, 1790*]. . . . As France has hitherto set the pattern to all Europe in matters of taste and fashion, so now she bids fair to afford a more noble example in science, liberty, and legislature [*November 4, 1790*]. Thus we have seen in the course of one year a complete regeneration of an immense empire. . . . Whatever may be the defects of the individual members of the National Assembly, we are at a loss to find in history a body of men who have displayed more courage, more wisdom, more firmness. [*But*] . . . the country is far from being in a state of tranquillity. The enemies of liberty are far too numerous and too daring not to excite commotions [*November 29, 1790*].

4. The New York *Daily Advertiser* (March 21, 1791)
on Burke's *Reflections:*
. . . the leading calumniator of the glorious French
Revolution . . . [*who*] views every transaction of the
National Assembly through the modicum of the grossest
prejudice in order to defend the rights of the corrupt
clergy of France. . . .

C. *Federalists versus Jefferson:*

1. From the *Diary of Gouverneur Morris* (November
19, 1790):
How will it all end? This unhappy country, bewildered
in the pursuit of metaphysical whimsies, presents to one's
moral view a mighty ruin. Like the remnants of ancient
magnificence, we admire the architecture of the temple,
while we detest the false god to whom it was dedicated.
Daws and ravens and the birds of night now build their
nests in its niches; the sovereign, humbled to the level
of a beggar's pity, without resources, without authority,
without a friend; the Assembly, at once a master and a
slave—new in power, wild in theory, raw in practice, it
engrosses all functions, though incapable of exercising
any, and has taken from this fierce, ferocious people
every restraint of religion and of respect. Here conjecture
may wander through unbounded space. What sum of
misery may be requisite to change popular will, calculation cannot determine. What circumstances may arise in
the order of Divine will to give direction to that will, our
sharpest vision cannot discover. What talents may be
found to seize those circumstances to influence that will,
and above all, to moderate the power which it must
confer, we are equally ignorant. One thing only seems to
be tolerably ascertained, that the glorious opportunity is
lost, and (for this time at least) the Revolution has failed.

2. John Adams to Dr. Price (April 19, 1790):
Accept my best thanks for your favor of February 1st
and the excellent discourse that came with it. I love the
zeal and spirit which dictated this discourse and admire
the general sentiments of it. From the year 1760 to this
hour, the whole scope of my life has been to support
such principles and propagate such sentiments. No sacri-

fices of myself or my family, no dangers, no labors have been too much for me in this great cause. The Revolution in France could not, therefore, be indifferent to me, but I have learned by awful experience to rejoice with trembling. I know that encyclopedists and economists, Diderot and D'Alembert, Voltaire and Rousseau, have contributed to this great event even more than Sidney, Locke or Hoadley, perhaps more than the American Revolution, and I own to you I know not what to make of a republic of thirty million atheists. . . . Too many Frenchmen, like too many Americans, pant for equality of persons and property. The impracticability of this God Almighty has decreed, and the advocates for liberty who attempt it will surely suffer for it.

3. From the *Journal* of Senator William Maclay (September 18, 1789):

By this and yesterday's papers, France seems travailing in the birth of freedom. Her throes and pangs of labor are violent. God give her a happy delivery! Royalty, nobility and vile pageantry, by which a few of the human race lord it over and tread on the necks of their fellow-mortals, seem likely to be demolished with their kindred Bastille, which is said to be laid in ashes. Ye gods! with what indignation do I review the late attempt of some creatures among us to revive this vile machinery! O Adams! Adams! what a wretch art thou!

4. Jefferson on the Federalists (letter of 1791):

Paine's pamphlet has been published and read with general applause here. . . . The Tory paper, Fenno's, rarely admits anything which defends the present form of government in opposition to his desire of subverting it to make way for a King, Lords and Commons. There are high names here in favor of the doctrine, but these publications have drawn forth pretty generally expressions of the public sentiment on this subject, and I thank God, they are to a man firm as a rock in their republicanism. [*In a note after the word "names," he added*]: Adams, Jay, Hamilton, Knox, and many of the Cincinnati. The second says nothing; the third is open. Both are dangerous. They pant after a union with England, as the power which is to support their projects, and are most determined anti-Gallicans. It is prognosticated that our re-

public is to end with the President's life, but I believe
they will find themselves all head and no body.

— Reading No. 9 =

THE ROAD TO WAR[9]

*The flight of the royal family was long and carefully
planned, as the letter of Marie Antoinette's friend, Count
Fersen, clearly indicates. During the suspension of Louis
XVI after the return from Varennes, the queen was still
instructing Fersen to urge the powers to issue a manifesto
without, however, going so far as to wage war against
the revolutionaries. The Feuillant leaders, meantime, were
rallying the Legislative Assembly to hold back the radical
and democratic agitation. The Declaration of Pillnitz
was Leopold's response to the appeals from France. While
Leopold's letter to Marie Antoinette in January, 1792,
discloses that he was still averse to war, Louis XVI, himself, was won over to the thought of military intervention
by Prussia and Austria. On the eve of war Marie Antoinette disclosed the general plan of campaign to the
Austrian ambassador. The Girondins, for their part,
actively preached a crusade against the "despots."*

1   1   1

[9] The following selections for (I) in this reading are all translated from the second volume of J. Jaurès, *Histoire so-
cialiste de la révolution française,* 8 vols. (Paris, 1922):
(I A), pp. 326-327; (I B), pp. 416-417; (I C), pp. 382-
383; (I D), p. 402. Reading (I E) is the translation from
F. M. Anderson, *op. cit.,* pp. 57-58. The selections in the
following group are translated from: (II A), Jaurès, *op.
cit.,* III, pp. 186-189; (II B), A. Malet and J. Isaac, *Révolution. Empire* (Paris, 1928), p. 116; (II C), Jaurès, *op.
cit.,* III, pp. 236-237; and (II D), *ibid.,* pp. 133-134.

I. The Flight of the King

A. *Count Fersen's Secret Letter Concerning the Flight of the Royal Family (March 7, 1791)*: All that I wrote to the King [*of Sweden*], as though the ideas were my own, about the flight of the King of France and the Queen of France, about the method of bringing about changes here and the necessity of foreign aid, is a plan already made and on which I am working. Nobody knows about it, and besides myself who am a foreigner, there are only four Frenchmen in the secret. The one who is in the secret and is most trustworthy is not in Paris [*General Bouillé*].

Be on your guard, particularly against all Frenchmen, even those who have the best intentions. . . . The Comte d'Artois and the Prince de Condé have nothing whatsoever to do with this plan. . . .

B. *Marie Antoinette's Instructions to Fersen (July 8, 1791)*: . . . The King thinks that the strait prison where he is held and the complete state of degradation to which the National Assembly has brought the Crown in no longer allowing it to act independently is well enough known by the foreign powers not to warrant any explanation here.

The King thinks that it is through the channel of negotiations alone that their help could be useful to him and his realm; that the military demonstration should be secondary and take place only if all paths of negotiation are blocked here.

The King thinks that open force, even after a first declaration, would be of incalculable danger, not only for himself and his family, but even for all the Frenchmen within the kingdom who do not follow in the path of the Revolution.

Résumé: He desires that the fact of the King's captivity be well established and well known to the foreign powers; he desires that the good will of his relatives, friends, and allies and other sovereigns who would wish to concur in its expression be made manifest by a kind of congress which would pursue the path of negotiations, with the understanding of course that there be an impressive military force to implement them; but always held in reserve so as not to give provocation for crime and massacre.

C. *Barnave's Speech (July 15, 1791) on the Dangers of Radicalism:* The facts have been very well established but I am taking them as a whole and I say: any change today is fatal; any prolongation of the Revolution today is disastrous. I am posing the question here, for it is here indeed that the national interest is involved. Are we going to end the Revolution? Are we going to begin it again? (Repeated applause.) If once you show distrust of the Constitution, at what point will you stop, and above all, at what point will our successors stop? . . .

A grave injury is being done us by perpetuating this revolutionary movement which has destroyed all there was to destroy and which has brought us to the point where we must stop. . . . Think, gentlemen, think of what will happen after you. You have done what is good for liberty, for equality; no arbitrary authority has been spared, no usurpation of self-esteem or of property rights has escaped; you have made all men equal before civil law and political law; you have recovered for and have restored to the state all that had been taken from it. Hence this great truth: if the Revolution takes one more step, it cannot do so without danger; hence, on the score of liberty, the first act that could follow would be the destruction of Royalty; hence, on the score of equality, the first step that could follow would be the destruction of property. (Applause.)

D. *Charles de Lameth (July 18, 1791) on the "Massacre" of the Champ-de-Mars:* The National Assembly has learned with grief that the enemies of the happiness and liberty of Frenchmen, usurping the mask, the language of patriotism, had misled some, had made them mutinous [*and*] rebels against the law, and had forced you [*the municipal authorities*] to take rigorous steps instead of those persuasive ones which up to now you have utilized with so much success.

The National Assembly approves your conduct and all

the measures you have taken; it notes with pleasure that the Parisian National Guard, soldiers of liberty and law and citizens . . . have in these circumstances given striking proof of their attachment to the Constitution and the law, and have continued to justify the high esteem and gratitude of the nation by their zeal, their moderation, and their loyalty. (Loud Applause.)

E. *The Declaration of Pillnitz* (*August 27, 1791*): His Majesty, the Emperor, and his Majesty, the King of Prussia, having given attention to the wishes and representatives of *Monsieur* (the brother of the King of France), and of M. le Comte d'Artois, jointly declare that they regard the present situation of his majesty the King of France, as a matter of common interest to all the sovereigns of Europe. They trust that this interest will not fail to be recognized by the powers, whose aid is solicited, and that in consequence they will not refuse to employ, in conjunction with their said majesties, the most efficient means in proportion to their resources to place the King of France in a position to establish with the most absolute freedom, the foundations of a monarchical form of government, which shall at once be in harmony with the rights of sovereigns and promote the welfare of the French nation. In that case [*Alors et dans ce cas*] their said majesties the Emperor and the King of Prussia are resolved to act promptly and in common accord with the forces necessary to obtain the desired common end.

In the meantime they will give such orders to their troops as are necessary in order that these may be in a position to be called into active service.

Leopold.
Frederick William.

II. The Warmongers

A. *Leopold to Marie Antoinette* (*January 31, 1792*): Dearest Sister, I can think of no better way to demonstrate my tender affection for you and the King during these critical times than by showing my feelings without the least reserve. I do so with the most whole-hearted cordiality by sending you this memorandum which serves as a reply to the one which you forwarded to me through the offices of the Comte de Mercy. . . .

Four months ago the Emperor shared the hope that time, aided by reason and experience alone, would suffice to effect amendments [*to the constitution*]. The secret communication herewith attached will prove the good faith with which, in accord with this hope, he seconded the resolution of the King and Queen. It is not for lack of effort on his part that the same views have not been adopted by all the courts as well as by the King's brothers and the émigrés.

It is not that the Emperor does not still persist in believing that the goal must and can be attained without disturbances and without war, because he is deeply convinced that nothing lasting can be effected except by conciliating the wishes and gaining the support of the most numerous class in the nation, composed of those who, wishing peace, order, and liberty, are also strongly attached to the monarchy. . . .

[*He then lays down the bases of a joint declaration by the powers.*]

The cause and the claims of the émigrés will not be supported; the internal affairs of France will not be interfered with by any active measure except if the safety of the King and his family be compromised by palpable new dangers and finally, that in no case will we aim at destroying the constitution but that we will limit ourselves to favoring its amendment in accordance with the above principles and by peaceful and conciliating means.

B. *Louis XVI to His Secret Agent Abroad* (*December 14, 1791*): Instead of a civil war, this will be a political war and things will be much better for it. . . . The physical and moral state of France makes it impossible for it to wage half a campaign, but I must act as though I were supporting war freely. . . . My conduct must be such that in misfortune the nation will see its only salvation in throwing itself into my arms.

C. *Marie Antoinette Discloses the Plan of the Campaign to the Austrian Ambassador* (*March 26, 1792*): M. Dumouriez, no longer in any doubt that the powers have agreed on military action, plans to begin here by an attack on Savoy at first and another on Liége. It is La Fayette's army presumably that will carry out this last-named attack. Here is the decision of yesterday's Council: It is well to know this plan so we can be on our guard and take all necessary measures. As it looks now, there will be no delay.

D. *Isnard, a Leading Girondin, Calls for a Crusade against "Tyrants":* Let us, on this occasion, rise to the full height of our mission. . . .

Let us say to Europe that the French would like peace but that if they are forced to draw the sword, they will cast away the scabbard and will not seek it again until they are crowned with the laurels of victory; and, even if they should be vanquished, their enemies would not enjoy their triumph, because they would rule only over dead men. (Applause.)

Let us say to Europe that we will respect the constitutions of all states, but that if the cabinets of foreign courts attempt to incite a war of kings against France, we will incite a war of the people against the kings. (Applause.)

Let us say to them that ten million Frenchmen, kindled by the fire of liberty, armed with the sword, with reason, with eloquence, would be able, if incensed, to change the face of the world and make the tyrants tremble on their thrones. . . .

— Reading No. 10 —

"THE DESPOTISM OF LIBERTY"[10]

[10] The selections in this reading are from: (I A, B), translation by F. M. Anderson, *op. cit.*, pp. 129-132; (II A), translation by J. H. Stewart, *op. cit.*, pp. 392-393 (reprinted by permission of The Macmillan Company); (II B), translated from P. de Vaissière (ed.), *Lettres d' "Aristocrates"* (Paris, 1907), pp. 476-477; (III A), translated from Prieur de la Côte d'Or, *Révélations sur le comité de salut public*, in G. Bouchard, *Un organisateur de la victoire, Prieur de la Côte d'Or, membre du comité de salut public* (Paris, 1946), pp. 438-439; (III B), translated from *Rapport et décrêt, du 23 août, l'an II de la République, sur la réquisition civique des jeunes citoyens pour la défense de la Patrie* (Paris, 1793), pp. 4-6; (III C), translation by F. M. Anderson, *op. cit.*, pp. 185-186; (III D), translated from Baron Frénilly, *Souvenirs*, as cited in G. Guénin and J. Nouaillac, *L'ancien régime et la révolution, 1715-1800* (Paris, 1921), pp. 302-303; (IV A), translated from M. Robespierre, *Rapport sur les principes de moralité publique* in *Moniteur*, No. 139 (February 7, 1794), pp. 561-564; (IV B), translation by F. M. Anderson, *op. cit.*, pp. 137-138; (IV C), translated from a report of the Committee of Public Safety, in F. A. Aulard, *Recueil des actes du comité de salut public*, 28 vols. (Paris, 1889-1951), XIII, p. 546; (IV D), translated from *Rapport fait à la Convention nationale . . . dans la séance du 13 prairial* (Paris, 1794), pp. 2-3, 3, 4, 5; (V A), translated from Thibaudeau, *Adresse à mes concitoyens, le 10 thermidor, an II*, cited in L. Jacob (ed.), *Robespierre vu par ses contemporains* (Paris, 1938), p. 184; (V B), translated from the report of a police observer, cited in F. A. Aulard, *Paris pendant la réaction thermidorienne*, 5 vols. (Paris, 1898-1902), I, p. 411; (V C), translated from *Mémoires du Colonel Pontbriand*, as cited in G. Guénin and J. Nouaillac, *op. cit.*, pp. 385-388.

The victories of the republican armies encouraged the deputies late in 1792 to extend and amplify their propaganda activities. After the king had been guillotined, the Convention issued a proclamation calling on all citizens to support it, but it is clear that the country was deeply divided. The bitter divisions within France and the reverses on the fighting front in 1793 brought the Revolution to the brink of defeat, from which it was saved by the "great" Committee of Public Safety. With the downfall of Robespierre on the 9th Thermidor (July 27, 1794), reaction set in against the committee and its rule.

✓   ✓   ✓

I. War and Propaganda

A. *Declaration for Assistance and Fraternity to Foreign Peoples (November 19, 1792)*: The National Convention declares, in the name of the French people, that it will accord fraternity and assistance to all peoples who shall wish to recover their liberty, and charges the executive power to give to the generals the necessary order to furnish assistance to these peoples and to defend the citizens who may have been or may be harassed for the cause of liberty. The present decree shall be translated and printed in all languages.

B. *Decree for Proclaiming the Liberty and Sovereignty of all Peoples (December 15, 1792)*: The National Convention, after having heard the report of its united committees of finances, war, and diplomacy, faithful to the principles of the sovereignty of the people, which do not permit it to recognize any of the institutions which bring an attack upon it, and wishing to settle the rules to be followed by the generals of the armies of the Republic in the countries where they shall carry its arms, decrees:

1. In the countries which are or shall be occupied by the armies of the Republic, the generals shall proclaim immediately, in the name of the French nation, the sovereignty of the people, the suppression of all the established authorities and of the existing imposts and taxes, the abolition of the tithe, of feudalism, of seigniorial rights, both feudal and *censuel,* fixed or precarious, of *banalities,*

of real and personal servitude of the privileges of hunting and fishing, of *corvées,* of the nobility, and generally of all privileges.

4. The generals shall directly place under the safeguard and protection of the French Republic all the movable and immovable goods belonging to the public treasury, to the prince, to his abettors, adherents and voluntary satellites, to the public establishments, to the lay and ecclesiastical bodies and communities; . . .

5. The provisional administration selected by the people shall be charged with the surveillance and control of the goods placed under the safeguard and protection of the French Republic; it shall look after the security of persons and property; . . .

11. The French nation declares that it will treat as enemies the people who, refusing liberty and equality, or renouncing them, may wish to preserve, recall, or treat with the prince and the privileged castes; it promises and engages not to subscribe to any treaty, and not to lay down its arms until after the establishment of the sovereignty and independence of the people whose territory the troops of the Republic have entered upon and who shall have adopted the principles of equality, and established a free and popular government.

II. The Guillotining of the King

A. *Proclamation of the Convention to the French People* (*January 23, 1793*) : Citizens, the tyrant is no more. For a long time the cries of the victims, whom war and domestic dissensions have spread over France and Europe, loudly protested his existence. He has paid his penalty, and only acclamations for the Republic and for liberty have been heard from the people.

We have had to combat inveterate prejudices, and the superstition of centuries concerning monarchy. Involuntary uncertainties and inevitable disturbances always accompany great changes and revolutions as profound as ours. This political crisis has suddenly surrounded us with contradictions and tumults.

. . . but the cause has ceased, and the motives have disappeared; respect for liberty of opinion must cause these tumultuous scenes to be forgotten; only the good which they have produced through the death of the tyrant and of tyranny now remains, and this judgment belongs in its entirety to each of us, just as it belongs to the entire nation. The National Convention and the French people are now to have only one mind, only one sentiment, that of liberty and civic fraternity.

Now, above all, we need peace in the interior of the Republic, and the most active surveillance of the domestic enemies of liberty. Never did circumstances more urgently require of all citizens the sacrifice of their passions and their personal opinions concerning the act of national justice which has just been effected. Today the French people can have no other passion than that for liberty.

Let us, through our union, avert the shame that domestic discord would bring upon our newborn republic. Let us, through our patriotism, avert those horrible shocks, those anarchical and disorderly movements which would soon overwhelm France with disturbances and grief, if our outside enemies, who are fomenting them, could profit therefrom. . . .

B. *An "Aristo" Reports on the Death of the King (January 23, 1793)*: Monsieur, . . . the frightful event of the 21st has spread dismay everywhere, and it is worth noting that even the most zealous partisans of the revolutionary system found this measure both excessive and dangerous. It will not save us from the untold ills which threaten us, the reality and duration of which are now all the more sure. Thus peace, security, fortune—one must make up one's mind to sacrificing all of these without hope of anything better. We must now see how the departments will look upon this and whether general approval there is as irresolute as in Paris, where it is supported by terror. I very much fear that civil war will come as a finishing touch to the abominable crimes and all the misfortunes which now assail us. I doubt, moreover, whether this crime, added to so many others, has the universal approval of France. Even if we thought that the king were guilty, we would not wish for his death, especially after his having endured so long and so sorrowful a captivity. . . . Meanwhile prudence must silence sensibility because under the empire of secret accusations, of inquisition, or even more, of tyranny, it is dangerous to speak one's thoughts. . . .

III. The Committee of Public Safety
Takes Command

A. *A Committee Member Describes How the Committee Worked:* Let us go on to the general sessions of the Committee. From seven o'clock in the morning, or even earlier, the most zealous betook themselves to their offices to read despatches, above all, those from the armies, or to prepare some special work. Around ten o'clock, the members present took up the business on hand, informally and freely discussing it, for there was never either a presiding officer or agenda or formal order of proceedings in the sessions. Decisions were soon reached and turned into resolutions in view of the unanimity of opinion on the political system to be followed and in view of their mutual confidence. At one o'clock, a few members would leave to attend the main session of the Convention, the others continued their business. They never postponed pressing matters but sometimes certain subjects were reserved for discussion before a member whose influence or knowledge were useful. Things went along like that until about five or six o'clock in the evening. Then they left to go out to dine . . . some snatching a hasty meal at a neighboring restaurant. Not later than eight o'clock, the meeting was resumed and continued into the night, most often until one or two in the morning. Two carriages brought the members home. It is worthy of note that the evening meetings were not interrupted by the absence of those who regularly attended the assembly of the Jacobins. Barère almost never went there any more; Carnot and Prieur de la Côte-d'Or, never. The last-named did not wish to affiliate themselves with this society in spite of several indirect bids; but their colleagues spoke of it not at all and did not seem to pay any attention to it.

From days spent thus, in scarcely a year an incredible mass of work emerged, thanks to the good will and to the energy of all members of the Committee, roused by the critical situation in France; thanks to the fearlessness with which they made use of the great powers in them invested. We can get an idea of their work from the impetus given to the fourteen armies of the Republic, comprising about 900,000 men, which had to be organized, led, and equipped with everything; by the suppression or the localization of the civil war in all parts of France; by the firm course that they imposed upon all administrative agencies; by the astonishing manufacture of arms and munitions of every kind and by the fine arts and public education institutions which were set up or planned; in short by the security and the confidence which it inspired within the National Assembly in spite of the agitation of factions within the country and the efforts of a leagued Europe against us.

B. *The Convention Proclaims a Levy-in-Mass* (*August 23, 1793*):

(*The excerpt that follows comes from the implementing report that the Committee of Public Safety drew up for the Convention. It was the most fervent expression of the new nationalism that inspired the revolutionaries.*)

The requisition of all resources is doubtless necessary, but it will be enough to use them gradually. Such is the sense of the levy of the entire population. All people are requisitioned, but all cannot go off to battle or perform the same functions.

Let us state a great truth: liberty has become the creditor of all citizens. Some owe it their labor, others their wealth, some their counsel, others the strength of their arms; all owe it the blood which flows in their veins Thus all the French, men and women alike, people of all ages, are summoned by the *Patrie* to defend liberty. All physical and moral faculties, all political and industrial means, belong to it by right; all metals, all elements, pay it their tribute Let everyone take up his post; let everyone behave ⸦ he should in this national and military uprising that the ending of the campaign demands of us, and all will soon be proud that they had worked together to save the *Patrie*. . . .

Thus all are requisitioned, but all will not march off to war. Some will make weapons, others will use them; some will prepare food supplies for combattants, others will sacrifice their clothing and what they most need themselves. Men, women, children, in requisitioning you the *Patrie* summons you all in the name of liberty and equality, and it designates to each of you according to his means the service he must give to the armies of the Republic.

Young men will fight, young men are called to conquer. Married men will forge arms, transport military baggage and guns and will prepare food supplies. Women, who at long last are to take their rightful place in the revolution and follow their true destiny, will forget their futile tasks: their delicate hands will work at making clothes for soldiers; they will make tents and they will extend their tender care to shelters where the defenders of the *Patrie* will receive the help that their wounds require. Children will make lint of old cloth. It is for them that we are fighting: children, those beings destined to gather all the fruits of the revolution, will raise their pure hands toward the skies. And old men, performing their missions again, as of yore, will be guided to the public squares of the cities where they will kindle the courage of young warriors and preach the doctrines of hate for kings and the unity of the Republic.

C. *The Law of Suspects* (*September 17, 1793*):

1. Immediately after the publication of the present decree all the suspect-persons who are in the territory of the Republic and who are still at liberty shall be placed under arrest.

2. These are accounted suspect-persons: 1st, those who by their conduct, their connections, their remarks or their writings show themselves the partisans of tyranny or federalism and the enemies of liberty; 2d, those who cannot, in the manner prescribed by the decree of March 21st last, justify their means of existence and the performance of their civic duties; 3d, those who have been refused certificates of civism; 4th, public functionaries suspended or removed from their functions by the National Convention or its commissioners and not reinstated, especially those who have been or shall be removed in virtue of the decree of August 14th last; 5th, those of the former nobles, all of the husbands, wives, fathers,

mothers, sons or daughters, brothers or sisters, and agents of the Emigrés who have not constantly manifested their attachment to the revolution; 6th, those who have emigrated from France in the interval from July 1, 1789, to the publication of the decree of March 30—April 8, 1792, although they may have returned to France within the period fixed by that decree or earlier.

3. The committees of surveillance established according to the decree of March 21st last, or those which have been substituted for them, either by the orders of the representatives of the people sent with the armies and into the departments, or in virtue of special decrees of the National Convention, are charged to prepare, each in its district, the list of suspect-persons, to issue warrants of arrest against them, and to cause seals to be put upon their papers. The commanders of the public force to whom these warrants shall be delivered shall be required to put them into execution immediately, under penalty of removal. . . .

D. *How Price Controls Worked: A Contemporary View of the Law of the Maximum (September 29, 1793)*: This law was the crowning touch to the general ill; until it was passed, even at the expense of ruining oneself, one could survive; one could buy a coat for a month's income and so forth. But after the publication of the Maximum, all merchandise disappeared as if by magic. One neither bought nor sold except on the sly; every purchase became a secret deal and one had to act fast. In the city of Paris alone there was an absolute shortage not only of bread, not only of fuel, but of all the necessities of life, while the countryside was glutted with the fruits of a good harvest. One had to live through those days when it was an indiscretion, an unheard of breach of good manners to dine with a friend without bringing one's own bread; when one met secretly to eat white bread which suspect pastry cooks ventured to make; when the bakers baked on order and with nothing but flour made of peas, vetch, or chestnuts which was distributed to them by the government; when at each baker's door, from dawn if not from the night before, long queues of the famished stood, losing a third of their day to get a piece of black, viscous bread. You had to be present or send someone to stand on these lines otherwise you were suspected of having bread at home and that was a crime which the government would have punished by a fine or the populace by pillage. Dozens of times, after getting this so-called bread which was brought to me, I hurled it against the wall where it stuck and even my dog never wanted to go near it. . . . The same scarcity extended to everything. One queued up for candles, soap, meat, wood, which each one of us got at the maximum price with a ration card issued by the section to buy at government-licensed shops. One saw the people of Paris take to the neighboring highways to bid for provisions which peasants displayed without bringing into the city for fear of the Maximum; and I recall having gone myself, during a terrible frost, as far as Charenton, to get hold of a little wagon of wood which I brought back across the fields to avoid any argument about it.

IV. The Committee of Public Safety Scans the Future

A. *Robespierre's Definition of the Goal of the Revolution (February 5, 1794)*: . . . We desire an order of things in which all base and cruel feelings are suppressed by the laws, and all beneficent and generous feelings evoked; in which ambition means the desire to merit glory and to serve one's country; in which distinctions arise only from equality itself; in which the citizen should submit to the magistrate, the magistrate to the people, the people to justice; in which the country assures the welfare of each individual, and each individual enjoys with pride the prosperity and glory of his country; in which all minds are enlarged by the continued conviction of republican sentiments and by the endeavor to win the respect of a great people; in which the arts adorn the liberty that ennobles them, and commerce is the source of public wealth, and not merely of monstrous opulence for a few families.

We desire to substitute in our country, morality for egoism, honesty for mere honor, principle for habit, duty for decorum, the empire of reason for the tyranny of fashion, contempt of vice for scorn of misfortune, pride for insolence, large-mindedness for vanity, the love of glory for the love of money, good men for "good company," merit for intrigue, genius for wit, truth for show, the charm of happiness for the dullness of pleasure, the grandeur of man for the pettiness of the so-called great, a people stout-hearted, powerful and happy for a people easygoing, frivolous and discontented—that is to say, all the virtues and the amazing achievements of the Republic for all the vices and puerilities of the monarchy. . . .

. . . We must crush both the internal and foreign enemies of the Republic, or perish with it. And in this situation, the first maxim of your policy should be to guide the people by reason and repress the enemies of the people by intimidation (*terreur*). If the mainspring of popular government during peace is virtue, the mainspring of popular government in rebellion is at once virtue and intimidation—virtue without which intimidation is disastrous, and intimidation, without which virtue is powerless. . . . Intimidation is merely justice—prompt, severe and inflexible. It is, therefore, an emanation of virtue; it is less a particular principle than a consequence of the general principles of democracy, applied to the most pressing needs of the country. . . .

We wish in short to fulfill the course of nature, to accomplish the destiny of mankind, to make good the promises of philosophy, to absolve Providence from the long reign of tyranny and crime. May France, illustrious formerly among peoples of slaves, eclipse the glory of all free peoples that have existed, become the model of nations, the terror of oppressors, the consolation of the oppressed, the adornment of the universe; and in sealing our wo.k with our blood may we ourselves at least see the dawn of universal happiness open before us! That is our ambition. That is our aim.

B. *Decree for Establishing the Worship of the Supreme Being* (*May 7, 1794*):

1. The French people recognize the existence of the Supreme Being and the immortality of the soul.

2. They recognize that the worship worthy of the Supreme Being is the practice of the duties of man.

3. They place in the first rank of these duties, to detest

bad faith and tyranny, to punish tyrants and traitors, to relieve the unfortunate, to respect the weak, to defend the oppressed, to do to others all the good that is possible and not to be unjust to anyone.

4. Festivals shall be instituted to remind man of the thought of the Divinity and of the dignity of his being.

5. They shall take their names from the glorious events of our Revolution, from the virtues most cherished and most useful to man, and from the great gifts of nature.

6. The French Republic shall celebrate every year the festivals of July 14, 1789, August 10, 1792, January 21, 1793, and May 31, 1793.

7. It shall celebrate on the days of decadi the list of festivals that follows: to the Supreme Being and to Nature; to the Human Race; to the French People; to the Benefactors of Humanity; to the Martyrs of Liberty; to Liberty and Equality; to the Republic; to the Liberty of the World; to the Love of the Fatherland; to the Hatred of Tyrants and of Traitors; to Truth; to Justice; to Modesty; to Glory and Immortality; to Friendship; to Frugality; to Courage; to Good Faith; to Heroism; to Disinterestedness; to Stoicism; to Love; to Conjugal Love; to Paternal Love; to Maternal Tenderness; to Filial Affection; to Childhood; to Youth; to Manhood; to Old Age; to Misfortune; to Agriculture; to Industry; to our Forefathers; to Posterity; to Happiness. . . .

C. *The Committee Drafts Poets for the Cause* (*May 16, 1794*): The Committee of Public Safety summons poets to celebrate the principal events of the French Revolution, to compose hymns and poems and republican dramas, to publicize the heroic deeds of the soldiers of liberty, the courage and loyalty of republicans, and the victories gained by French arms. It also summons citizens who cultivate letters to preserve for posterity the most noteworthy facts and great epochs in the renascence of the French people, to give to history that firm and stern character which befits the annals of a great people engaged in winning the liberty which all the tyrants of Europe are attacking. It bids them to write classic works and to inject republican morality into works intended for public instruction, while the Committee will be preparing for the Convention a type of national award to be decreed for their labors, and the date and form of the competition.

D. *Indoctrinating the Youth: The Report of the Committee of Public Safety on Revolutionary Education* (*June 1, 1794*): What is involved here is the procedure that must be followed quickly to rear truly republican defenders of the *Patrie* and to revolutionize the youth as we have revolutionized the armies. What is involved is the question of speeding learning and public military instruction. It is a matter of proving to the cold and methodical minds of men who weigh all teaching procedures slowly that the time is past for opposing old habits to principles and principles to the revolution.

. . . It is when man begins to be enlightened by reason, when understanding re-enforces his strength, that the *Patrie* should take him in hand. The young man of sixteen, seventeen, or seventeen and a half, is best prepared to receive a republican education. Nature's work is accomplished. At that moment the *Patrie* asks each citizen: What will you do for me? What means will you employ to defend my unity and my laws, my territory and my independence?

The Convention gives its reply to the *Patrie* today, a School of Mars is going to open its doors. Three thousand young citizens, the strongest, the most intelligent and the most exemplary in conduct, are going to attend this new establishment. Three thousand children of worthy parents are going to devote themselves to common tasks, to fashion themselves for military service. They will come from the heart of the new generation . . . to dedicate their nightly toil and their blood to their country. . . .

Love for the *Patrie,* this pure and generous sentiment which knows no sacrifice that it cannot make . . . ; love for the *Patrie* which was only a myth in the monarchies and which has covered the annals of the Republic with heroism and virtue, will become the ruling passion of the pupils of the School of Mars. . . .

In founding this fine revolutionary establishment, the National Convention ought thus to address the families of the *sans-culottes* and the young citizens whom it calls to the School of Mars: "Citizens, for too long has ignorance dwelt in the countryside and the workshops; for too long have fanaticism and tyranny prevailed over the first thoughts of young citizens to enslave them or arrest their development. It is not for slaves or mercenaries to rear free men; it is the *Patrie* itself which today assumes this important function, which it will never relinquish to prejudice, calculation, and aristocracy. Loyalty to your own families must end when the great family calls you. The Republic leaves to parents the guidance of your first years, but as soon as your intelligence develops, it loudly proclaims the right it has over you. You are born for the Republic and not to be the pride of family despotism or its victims. It takes you at that happy age when your ardent feelings go out to virtue and respond naturally to enthusiasm for the good of and love for the *Patrie*.

V. The Thermidorian Reaction

A. *Vilifying Robespierre: One of His Fellow Deputies Explains Why Robespierre Was Overthrown:* The tyrant is no more. Robespierre has just died the death of traitors. His accomplices have perished with him and liberty is triumphant. *Patrie*, Probity, Truth, your sacred names will no longer be sullied by lewd lips; your reign will bring back to Frenchmen, confidence, fraternity and happiness. Oppression has ended. Patriots, breathe, emulate your representatives; behave again like republicans.

For several months a single man, strengthened by usurped popularity and enormous influence, ruled like a despot over the government or blocked its course; tyrannized the Convention or debased it; raised himself above the law or shamelessly dictated it; made himself master of public opinion or destroyed it to replace it with his own; oppressed patriots and prescribed everything that had integrity and virtue; set up tribunals and dictated their verdicts to them; protected scoundrels and intriguers; filled the offices of constituted authorities with his creatures; in this way seized civil and military power to make them serve his whims and furies. In brief, Robespierre had aroused dark suspicion, cruel distrust, alarms, terror in all hearts; he had separated man from man and carried out this maxim of all tyrants: divide and rule. The proscription lists, spying, defamation, fanaticism, all was in his corrupt hands a legitimate means of immolating the defenders of the rights of the people and of establishing tyranny, but the spirit of liberty still watched over this generous nation, immortalized by five years of toil, sacrifice and combat. The throne of the usurper has vanished to yield to the scaffold.

B. *Attacking the Cult of Marat: A Police Report* (*January 20, 1795*): Yesterday the day passed in the greatest calm until six or seven in the evening when some young men, frequenters of the Cafe de Chartres, met as they had planned. One of them spoke up and said: "I just dined at Février's with my brothers of the Faubourg St. Antoine; they will be around with the mannikin in ten minutes." A short time later, two or three hundred people assembled in the Jardin-Egalité with a mannikin which they called "Jacobin," wearing a black wig and red bonnet on its head, [*and carrying*] a purse and portfolio in one hand, a torch in the other. In the midst of this mob, lit up by a half-dozen torches, one of them made a speech and then sang several songs while the audience, as chorus, repeated the refrain; from there they left en masse and betook themselves first, and with much clamor, on the route to the Place de la Réunion, where they insulted the memory of Marat; from there to the court before [*the convent of*] the Jacobins where the mannikin was burnt. The ashes were then tossed into a chamber pot and thrown into the Montmartre sewer, the place, they said, which ought to be the Pantheon of all Jacobins and bloodsuckers. One citizen to whom this behavior appeared, at the least, dangerous, spoke her mind somewhat loudly; she was whipped with great indecency after the most horrible revilement. . . .

C. *The Religious War in Brittany: Recollections of a Counter-Revolutionary:* One of Colonel de Pontbriand's soldiers asked him for permission to go to see his father in the town of Prince; he gave it to him reluctantly, because he had been warned that there were enemies in Juvigné and enjoined him not to sleep in the town if the news were true. The soldier promised but nevertheless

stayed on despite [*the protests of*] his parents. He had
been gone for three hours when at about ten o'clock at
night, the town was invaded by three hundred men. The
republicans entered his home where he was taken prisoner. His musket was beside him. He was treated with
unexampled barbarity; they burned his feet in his father's
presence and pulled them out of the fire only when he
lost consciousness; then they forced him to drink a glass
of brandy to revive him and then began that horrible
torture again. His sufferings lasted all night; the unfortunate creature said nothing more, while he had the
strength to speak but: "My God, it is for you, it is for
my religion that I have been fighting. My God, have pity
upon me. My sufferings are for you." He did not utter a
groan or shed a tear; his father and the other people in
the house shrieked lamentably, several soldiers themselves
wept and left after having implored their comrades in
vain to finish off the wretch quickly. About three in the
morning this troop left for Prince. Several soldiers carried the half-dead man up to a calvary near the town,
on the road to Dompierre-du-Chemin; one of them then
said: "He kept telling us all night that he was fighting
for his God, let him die for his God. Let us crucify him."
The horrible advice would have been followed and acted
upon by his comrades save for the unexpected arrival of
an officer with some regulars whom he commanded to
shoot him. The territorial guards cast themselves upon
the corpse and pierced it with so many bayonet wounds
that it was unrecognizable. The officer released the father
whom they had dragged there; he told him that he had
been unaware of what had been happening at his home,
that he was in despair over it and that he would have
stopped it.

— Reading No. 11 —

ENGLAND AND AMERICA, 1793-1799 [11]

William Pitt had pursued a policy of neutrality in the first years of the Revolution, but by the end of 1792 considerations of national interest swung him over to believing that England could not escape war. The war turned public opinion sharply against France, but the prorevolutionary societies and men in public life, like Charles James Fox, resisted the current and defended the constitutional rights of English citizens. Opinion in the United States remained favorable to France longer than it did in England, but the tide of feeling turned by 1794, and for the remainder of the decade the conservative forces were in the ascendancy.

✓   ✓   ✓

[11] Reading (I A) is an extract from Pitt's Speech of February 1, 1793, in which he prepares his country for war. It comes from W. Cobbett (ed.), *Parliamentary History of England* . . . , 36 vols. (London, 1806-1820), XXX, pp. 278-283; (I B), from W. Cobbett, T. B. Howell, and T. S. Howell (eds.), *Complete Collection of State Trials*, 33 vols. (London, 1809-1828), XXIII, p. 766; (I C), *ibid.*, XXV, pp. 640-644; (I D), from W. Cobbett, *op. cit.*, XXXIII, pp. 621-622; (II A) is from the *Columbian Centinel* (January 9, 1793); (II B), from E. P. Link, *Democratic-Republican Societies, 1790-1800* (New York, 1942), p. 11 (reprinted by permission of the Columbia University Press); (II C), from *National Gazette* (Philadelphia, May 22, 1793); (II D), from C. D. Hazen, *op. cit.*, p. 245; (II E), *ibid.*, pp. 297-298.

I. The Reaction in England

A. *Pitt Prepares the English for War: His Speech in Commons (February 1, 1793)*: Their decree of the 15th of December contains a fair illustration and confirmation of their principles and designs. . . . Whenever they obtain a temporary success, whatever be the situation of the country into which they come, . . . they have determined not to abandon the possession of it, till they have effected the utter and absolute subversion of its form of government, of every ancient, every established usage, however long they may have existed, and however much they may have been revered. They will not accept, under the name of liberty, any model of government, but that which is conformable to their own opinions and ideas. . . . They have regularly and boldly avowed these instructions, which they sent to the commissioners who were to carry these orders into execution. . . . They have stated, that they would organize every country by a disorganizing principle; and afterwards, they tell you all this is done by the will of the people. . . . And then comes this plain question, what is this will of the people? It is the power of the French. They have explained what that liberty is which they wish to give to every nation; and if they will not accept of it voluntarily, they compel them. They take every opportunity to destroy every institution that is most sacred and most valuable in every nation where their armies have made their appearance; and under the name of liberty, they have resolved to make every country in substance, if not a form, a province dependent on themselves, through the despotism of Jacobin societies. We see, therefore, that France has trampled under foot all laws, human and divine. She has at last avowed the most insatiable ambition, and greatest contempt for the law of nations, which all independent states have hitherto professed most religiously to observe; and unless she is stopped in her career, all Europe must soon learn their ideas of justice . . . and principles of liberty from the mouth of the French cannon.

I would next proceed to their confirmed pledge, not to interfere in the government of other neutral countries. . . . I need not remind the house of the decree of the 19th,

November, which is a direct attack on every government in Europe, by encouraging the seditious of all nations to rise up against their lawful rulers, and by promising them their support and assistance. By this decree, they hold out an encouragement to insurrection and rebellion in every country in the world. They show you they mean no exception, by ordering this decree to be printed in all languages. . . . And therefore I might ask any man of common sense . . . whether it was not meant to extend to England, whatever might be their pretences to the contrary? . . .

To all this I shall only observe, that in the whole context of their language, on every occasion, they show the clearest intention to propagate their principles all over the world. . . . They have proscribed royalty as a crime, and will not be satisfied but with its total destruction. The dreadful sentence which they have executed on their own unfortunate monarch, applies to every sovereign now existing.

France can have no right to annul the stipulations relative to the Scheldt, unless she has also the right to set aside, equally, all the other treaties between all the powers of Europe, and all the other rights of England, or of her allies. England will never consent that France shall arrogate the power of annulling at her pleasure, and under the pretence of a natural right of which she makes herself the only judge, the political system of Europe, established by solemn treaties, and guaranteed by the consent of all the powers. Such a violation of rights as France has been guilty of, it would be difficult to find in the history of the world. The conduct of that nation is in the highest degree arbitrary, capricious, and founded upon no one principle of reason and justice.

B. *Lord Justice Braxfield, Addressing the Jury on the Trial of Maurice Margot*[12] *at Edinburgh* (*January 13-14, 1794*): But gentlemen, in order to constitute the crime of sedition, it is not necessary that the meeting should have

---

[12] Maurice Margot was a Frenchman by birth who was sent as a delegate to Edinburgh by the London Corresponding Society. Lord Braxfield sentenced him to fourteen years' transportation to Botany Bay.

had in view to overturn the constitution by mobs and by violence to overturn the king and parliament. For I apprehend, in some sense, the crime of sedition consists in poisoning the minds of the lieges, which may naturally in the end have a tendency to promote violence against the state; and endeavouring to create a dissatisfaction in the country, which nobody can tell where it will end, it will very naturally end in overt rebellion; and if it has that tendency, though not in the view of the parties at the time, yet if they have been guilty of poisoning the minds of the lieges, I apprehend that that will constitute the crime of sedition to all intents and purposes. Now, gentlemen, take a view of the conduct of this meeting, and attend to the time when all this reform, and all this noise and declamation is made against the constitution. It is at a time when we are at war with a great nation, a cruel ferocious nation, that requires all our strength, and not only our strength, but the strength of all our allies to get the better of them; and the greatest unanimity is necessary. I submit to you whether a man that wishes well to his country, would come forward and insist upon a reform, parliamentary or not parliamentary, at such a crisis; which would create discontent in the minds of the people, when every good subject would promote unanimity among the lieges to meet the common enemy. I say in place of that, to bring forward a great reform in parliament is a thing totally inconsistent with the constitution of this country. I say, bringing it forward at that period is a strong proof that they were not well-wishers to the constitution, but enemies to it. I say that no good member of society would have taken those measures. I appeal to you all, that you are living under a happy government in peace and plenty, in perfect security of your lives and property, the happiest nation upon the face of the earth; and when that is the situation of this country, I appeal to you whether I have not given a fair and just description of it: for a set of men in that situation to raise a faction in the minds of the lower order of the people, and create disaffection to the government, and consequently make a division in that country; . . . I say, these things appear to be from the very conjuncture at which they are brought forward, sedition of a very high nature.

C. *The London Corresponding Society Protests to the People of Great Britain and Ireland over the Unfair Trial of John Horne Tooke (January 20, 1794)*:

At a General Meeting
of the
LONDON CORRESPONDING SOCIETY
HELD AT THE GLOBE TAVERN, STRAND,
On Monday, the 20th Day of January, 1794.
Citizen John Martin, in the Chair,
The following Address to the People of Great
Britain and Ireland was read and agreed to.

CITIZENS;—We have referred to *Magna Charta,* to the *Bill of Rights,* and to the Revolution and we certainly do find that our ancestors did establish wise and wholesome laws; but we do certainly find, that, of the venerable Constitution of our ancestors, hardly a vestige remains.

Can you believe that those who send virtuous Irishmen, and Scotchmen fettered with felons to Botany Bay, do not meditate and will not attempt to seize the first moment to send us after them? Or, if we had not just cause to apprehend the same inhuman treatment; if instead of the most imminent danger, we were in perfect safety from it; should we not disdain to enjoy any liberty or privilege whatever, in which our honest Irish and Scotch brethren did not equally and as fully participate with us? Their cause then and ours is the same. And it is both our duty and our interest to stand or fall together. The Irish parliament and the Scotch judges, actuated by the same English influence, have brought us directly to the point. There is no further step beyond that which they have taken. We are at issue. We must now choose at once either liberty or slavery for ourselves and our posterity. Will you wait till BARRACKS are erected in every village, and till subsidized Hessians and Hanoverians are upon us?

You may ask, perhaps, by what means shall we seek redress?

We answer, that men in a state of civilized society are bound to seek redress of the grievances from the laws; as long as any redress can be obtained by the laws. But our common Master whom we serve (whose law is a law of liberty, and whose service is perfect freedom) has taught us not to expect to gather grapes from thorns, nor figs from thistles. We must have redress from our own laws and not from the laws of our plunderers, enemies, and oppressors.

THERE IS NO REDRESS FOR A NATION CIR-CUMSTANCED AS WE ARE, BUT IN A FAIR, FREE, AND FULL REPRESENTATION OF THE PEOPLE.

J. MARTIN, CHAIRMAN
T. HARDY, SECRETARY

D. *Charles James Fox Moves the Repeal of the Treason and Sedition Acts (May 19, 1797)*: In proportion as opinions are open, they are innocent and harmless. Opinions become dangerous to a state only when persecution makes it necessary for the people to communicate their ideas under the bond of secrecy. Do you believe it possible that the calamity which now rages in Ireland would have come to its present heights, if the people had been allowed to meet and divulge their grievances? Publicity makes it impossible for artifice to succeed, and designs of a hostile nature lose their danger by the certainty of exposure. But it is said that these bills will expire in a few years; that they will expire when we shall have peace and tranquillity restored to us. What a sentiment to inculcate! You will tell the people, that when everything goes well, when they are happy and comfortable, then they may meet freely, to recognize their happiness, and pass eulogiums on their government; but that in a moment of war and calamity, of distrust and misconduct, it is not permitted them to meet together, because then, instead of eulogizing, they might think proper to condemn ministers. What a mockery is this! What a mockery is this! What an insult to say that this is preserving to the people the right of petition! To tell them that they shall have a right to applaud, a right to rejoice, a right to meet when they are happy, but not a right to condemn, not a right to deplore their misfortunes, not a right to suggest a remedy! I hate these insidious modes of undermining and libelling the constitution of the country. If you mean to say, that the mixed and balanced government of England is good only for holidays and sunshine, but that it is inapplicable to a day of dis-

tress and difficulty, say so. If you mean that freedom is
not as conducive to order and strength as it is to happiness,
say so; and I will enter the lists with you, and contend,
that among all the other advantages arising from liberty,
are the advantages of order and strength in a supereminent
degree, and that too, in the moment when they are most
wanted. Liberty is order. Liberty is strength. Good God,
Sir, am I, on this day, to be called upon to illustrate the
glorious and soothing doctrine? Look round the world
and admire, as you must, the instructive spectacle! You
will see that liberty not only is power and order, but that
it is power and order predominant and invincible; that it
derides all other sources of strength; that the heart of
man has no impulse, and can have none that dares to
stand in competition with it; and if, as Englishmen, we
know how to respect its value, surely the present is the
moment of all others, when we ought to secure its invigor-
ating alliance.

II. The United States: Pro and Con

A. *The Tammany Society of New York Celebrates the
Victories of the French Republican Troops* (*December
27, 1792*):

> By hell inspir'd with brutal rage,
> Austria and Prussia both engage,
> To crush fair freedom's flame;
> But the intrepid sons of France
> Have led them such a glorious dance
> They've turned their backs for shame
>
> May heaven continue still to bless
> The arms of freedom with success
> Till tyrants are no more;
> And still as Gallia's sons shall fly
> From victory to victory,
> We'll, shouting, cry Encore! . . .

B. *The Democratic Society of Pennsylvania Sends a Cir-
cular Expounding the Principles of Popular Sovereignty*
(*1793*): We have the pleasure to communicate to you a
copy of the constitution of the Democratic Society in

hopes that after a candid consideration of its principles, and objects, you may be induced to promote its adoption in the county of which you are an inhabitant.

Every mind, capable of reflection, must perceive, that the present crisis in the politics of nations is peculiarly interesting to America. The European Confederacy, transcendent in power, and unparalleled in iniquity, menaces the very existence of freedom. Already its baneful operation may be traced in the tyrannical destruction of the Constitution of Poland; and should the glorious efforts of France be eventually defeated, we have reason to presume, that, for the consummation of monarchical ambition, and the security of its establishments, this country, the only remaining depository of liberty, will not long be permitted to enjoy in peace, the honors of an independent, and the happiness of a republican government.

Nor are the dangers arising from a foreign source the only causes at this time, of apprehension and solicitude. The seeds of luxury appear to have taken root in our domestic soil; and the jealous eye of patriotism of wealth and the arrogance of power.

This general view of our situation has led to the institution of the Democratic Society. A constant circulation of useful information, and a liberal communication of republican sentiments, were thought to be the best antidotes to any political poison, with which the vital principles of civil liberty might be attacked; for by such means, a fraternal confidence will be studiously marked; and a standard will be erected, to which, in danger and distress, the friends of liberty may successfully resort.

To obtain these objects, then, and to cultivate on all occasions the love of peace, order, and harmony; an attachment to the constitution and a respect to the laws of our country will be the aim of the Democratic Society.

C. *A Committee of Prominent Philadelphia Citizens Extends Welcome to "Citizen" Genêt (May, 1793)*: For such reasons, sir, we have been naturally led to contemplate the struggles of France with a fraternal eye, sympathizing in all her calamities, and exulting in all her successes; but there is another interest, the interest of freedom and equality, which adds to the force of our affections and renders the cause of France important to every republic and dear to all the human race.

Be assured, therefore, that justly regarding the cultivation of republican principles as the best security for the permanency of our own popular governments, we rest our favorite hopes at this momentous crisis on the conduct of the French; and earnestly giving to the national exertions our wishes and our prayers, we cannot resist the pleasing hope that, although America is not a party in the existing war, she may still be able in a state of peace to demonstrate the sincerity of her friendship by affording every useful assistance to the citizens of her sister republic.

D. *Congressman William Smith Decries Revolutionary Excesses* (*July 4, 1796*) *at Charleston, South Carolina:* Through the wondrous meanderings of her stupendous revolution, how we rejoiced to see her combating and crushing the hydra of her ancient despotism. How have we mourned to see the brilliant prospect oft o'erclouded and the hydra of popular tyranny springing up in its place. . . . In tracing the rise and progress of this astonishing revolution the humane American must wish to draw a veil over the mournful scenes which have tarnished so bright an epoch of modern history. But have not even they their use? Will they not impress on our minds more forcibly than all the precepts of moralists the dire effects of the prostration of religion, government and law? . . . At the recital of such atrocities human nature stands confounded. Should they be hereafter recorded by the faithful historian, Liberty, appalled, will turn from them with horror, and outraged Humanity, in tears, will snatch the crimsoned page from the polluted volume.

E. *A Federalist Writer, Robert Treat Paine, Deplores the Moral Irresponsibility of the French Republicans* (*1799*): The French Republick has exhibited all the vices of civilization without one of the virtues of barbarism. . . . Political empiricism has never attained in any age or nation so universal an ascendency as at the present day in the "Illuminated Republick." Unfettered by the fear of innovation, and unshackled by the prejudice of ages, the modern Frenchman is educated in a system of moral and religious chimeras, which dazzle by their novelty those volatile intellects, which prescriptive wisdom could never impress with veneration. Every Frenchman who has read a little is a pedant; and the whole race of these horn-book philosophers is content with the atheism of Mirabeau, the historick pages of Rollin and Plutarch, the absurd philanthropy of Condorcet, and the visionary politics of Rousseau. These are the boundaries of their literary ambition, of their political science. [*Turning to the influence of the Revolution in America*]: Who does not remember the letter to Mazzei or the arrival of Genêt? Who has forgotten that dubious era in our history when illuminated fraternities were scattered, like the pestiferous effluvia of the poison-tree of Java, from Altamaha to St. Croix? When anarchy and disorganization were the order of the day and French consuls and French assignats the order of the night? When our "civick feasts" were introduced to celebrate French victories and our "watermelon frolicks" to disseminate French principles? When political infidelity was a paramount title to the suffrages of the people? When Foreign Influence, like the golden calf, seduced multitudes from the worship of true liberty!

— Reading No. 12 —

THE MIDDLE CLASS REPUBLIC [13]

When the Constitution of the Year III [1795] was voted, the Convention came to an end and a constitutional regime was reestablished. The first act of the Directors was to issue a manifesto to the citizens asking them to support the new government. But the Executive Directory was unable to solve the many grave problems it had inherited, among those the religious and economic problems. It was overthrown by Bonaparte, who formally proclaimed to the French people that the Revolution was ended.

✓   ✓   ✓

I. The Manifesto of the Directors (November 5, 1795)

Frenchmen, the Executive Directory has just been installed.

Resolved to maintain liberty or to perish, we are determined to consolidate the Republic and to govern vigorously and speedily under the provisions of the Constitution.

Republicans, place your trust in it; its destiny will never be separated from yours; inflexible justice and the strictest observance of laws will guide it. To wage active war on royalism, to revive patriotism, to repress all fac-

[13] The first selection in these readings is translated from *Moniteur* (November 10, 1795); (II), is translated from Babeuf's *Le Tribun du Peuple* (November 30, 1795), pp. 83-107; (III), is a translation by F. M. Anderson, *op. cit.*, pp. 140-141; (IV), is translated from *Correspondance de Napoléon Ier*, 32 vols. (Paris, 1858-1870), **VI**, p. 25.

tions vigorously, to destroy all factional spirit, and vanquish all desire for vengeance, to establish concord, to restore peace, to regenerate morals, to reopen the sources of production, to revive commerce and industry, to crush speculation, to give new life to the arts and sciences, to re-establish plenty and the public credit, to restore social order for the chaos which is inseparable from revolutions, in a word, to give the French Republic the happiness and glory which it awaits—such is the task of your legislators and of the Executive Directory. . . .

Wise laws, promptly and vigorously enforced, will soon make us forget our protracted sufferings.

But so many evils cannot be atoned nor so much good accomplished in a day. The French people are just and upright; they will see that . . . we need time, calm, patience, and confidence equal to the efforts we have to make. Such confidence will not be betrayed if the people no longer allow themselves to give heed to the perfidious suggestions of royalists who are renewing their plots, of fanatics who tirelessly inflame the minds of people, and of leeches who do not fail to take advantage of our sad plight.

It will not be betrayed if the people do not blame the new authorities for the disorders caused by six years of revolution, which can be expiated only with time; it will not be betrayed if the people recall that, for more than three years, whenever the enemies of the Republic . . . provoked disturbances, . . . such disturbances served only to further discredit us and to impede production and plenty, which only order and public tranquillity can produce.

Frenchmen, you will not hamper a newborn government . . . ; but you will wisely support the active efforts and the calm progress of the Executive Directory in the prompt establishment of public happiness; and without fail will soon bring about national peace and prosperity.

II. Babeuf Expounds the Principles of Utopian Communism (November 30, 1795)

(Babeuf was a minor government official who organized his small group of followers into a "Society of Equals."

The Directory suppressed the society; and Babeuf was arrested, brought to trial and condemned to death.)

It is time to speak of democracy itself, to define what we mean by it and what we wish it to give us; and in concert with the common people, to devise ways of instituting and maintaining it. . . . We have shown that since '89, and especially since '94 and '95, the mass of public suffering and oppression has made more pressing than ever before the mighty uprising of the people against their oppressors. . . . Shielded by our hundred thousand swords and our impassioned words, we shall proclaim the true first code of nature which should never have been broken.

. . . It is clear that everything that men own over and above their individual proportional share in the goods of society is theft and usurpation.

That it is therefore just to take it away from them. . . .

That the products of industry and talent also become the property of all . . . because they are only a compensation for the preceding inventions of industry and talent from which these inventors and workers have profited. . . .

That education is a monstrosity when it is unequal, when it is the exclusive inheritance of one group of society; when in the hands of that group it becomes a stock machine, a depot of weapons of all sorts, with the help of which it fights the other group which is unarmed and which, consequently, it easily succeeds in strangling, deceiving, stripping and enslaving. . . .

That social institutions must bring us to this point of depriving every individual of the hope of ever becoming either richer, or more powerful, or more outstanding through his learning, than any of his equals. . . .

That the sole means of reaching that point is to establish a communal form of administration; to abolish private property; to have each man develop the skill and pursue the activity of which he is capable; to oblige him to deposit the fruit [*of his work*] in a common storehouse; and to set up a simple distributing agency, a food administration which, on the basis of a register of all individuals and all products will allocate the latter with the most scrupulous equality . . . to each citizen. . . .

That this government will do away with all landmarks, hedgerows, walls, locks, disputes, legal trials, thefts, assassinations, all crimes; courts, prisons, scaffolds, sorrows and despair caused these calamities; envy, jealousy, insatiable greed, arrogance, deceit, duplicity, in short, all Vices; in addition—and this doubtless is the esential point—[*it will do away with*] the gnawing worm of general, individual, and perpetual anxiety which each one of us has about our fate for the morrow, the next month, the next year, about our old age, our children, and their children.

Such is the summary of the awe-inspiring Manifesto which we will offer the oppressed masses of the French people. . . . People, awake to hope; . . . Rejoice in the vision of a happy future.

III. Organic Act upon Religion (September 29, 1795)

. . . Considering that by the terms of the Constitution, nobody can be prevented from exercising, in conformity with the laws, the worship which he has chosen; that nobody can be forced to contribute to the expenses of any sect, and that the Republic does not pay salaries for any of them;

Considering that, these fundamental bases of the free exercise of worship being thus laid down, it is important, on the one hand, to reduce into laws the necessary consequences which are derived therefrom, and, for that purpose, to unite them into a single body and to modify or complete those which have been rendered; and, on the other hand, to add to them the penal provisions which may assure the execution of them;

Considering that the laws to which it is necessary to conform in the exercise of worship do not legislate upon what belongs to the domain of thought only, or upon the relations of man with the objects of his worship, and that they have and can have for their purpose only a surveillance restricted to measures of police and public security;

That thus they ought to guarantee to free exercise of worship by the punishment of those who disturb the ceremonies or outrage the ministers in their functions;

To demand of the ministers of every sect a purely civic guarantee against the abuse which they may make of their ministry in order to excite disobedience to the laws of the State;

To anticipate, prevent, or punish everything which may tend to render a sect exclusive or dominant and persecuting, such as acts of the communes in the collective name, endowments, forced contributions, acts of violence relative to the expenses of sects, the exposure of special symbols in certain places, the exercise of ceremonies and the use of costumes outside of the premises designated for the said exercises, and the undertakings of the ministers relative to the civil condition of the citizens;

To repress offences which may be committed by occasion or abuse of the exercise of worship, . . . [*The terms of the decree by which the state ended its responsibility for maintaining religious worship then follow.*]

IV. Proclamation of the Consuls to the French People
(December 15, 1799)

Frenchmen!

A Constitution is herewith presented to you.

It ends the uncertainties which the provisional government introduced into foreign affairs and into the domestic and military situation of the Republic.

In the institutions which it establishes, it puts at the head magistrates whose devotion seemed necessary for its successful creation.

The Constitution is founded on the true principles of representative government, on the sacred rights of property, equality, and liberty.

The powers which it institutes will be strong and stable, as they have to be in order to guarantee the rights of citizens and the interests of the state.

Citizens, the Revolution is established on the principles upon which it was founded: it is over.

BIBLIOGRAPHY

Of the many French works not translated, the reader's attention is called only to the following: Georges Lefebvre, *La Révolution française* (Paris, 1951), a penetrating and brilliant history; Jacques Godechot, *Les Institutions de la France sous la Révolution et l'Empire* (Paris, 1951), a valuable work of reference; Albert Sorel, *L'Europe et la Révolution française.* 8 vols. (Paris, 1895-1904), although outmoded, still the basic study of the impact of the Revolution outside France;[1] and E. Labrousse, *La crise de l'économie française à la fin de l'Ancien Régime et au début de la Révolution* (Paris, 1943).

GENERAL ACCOUNTS

Brinton, C., *A Decade of Revolution, 1789-1799* (1934).

Madelin, L., *The French Revolution* (1917).

Mathiez, A., *The French Revolution* (1928).

Thompson, J. M., *The French Revolution* (Oxford, 1943).

COLLECTIONS OF DOCUMENTS

Anderson, F. M., *Constitutions and other Select Documents Illustrative of the History of France, 1789-1901* (Minn., 1904).

Stewart, J. H., *A Documentary Survey of the French Revolution* (1951).

THE OLD REGIME

Barber, E. G., *The Bourgeoisie in 18th Century France* (Princeton, 1955).

---

[1] J. Godechot's remarkable study, *La Grande Nation. L'Expansion révolutionnaire de la France dans le monde, 1789-1799*, 2 vols. (Paris, 1956), appeared too late to be utilized for this book.

Hyslop, B. F., *A Guide to the General Cahiers of 1789* (1936).

Lefebvre, G., *The Coming of the French Revolution* (Princeton, 1947).

Martin, K., *French Liberal Thought in the Eighteenth Century* (1929).

Sée, H., *Economic and Social Conditions in France during the Eighteenth Century* (1927).

BIOGRAPHIES AND SPECIAL STUDIES

Barthou, L., *Mirabeau* (1913).

Bradby, E. D., *Barnave*. 2 vols. (1915).

Brinton, C., *The Jacobins* (1930).

Bruun, G., *Saint-Just. Apostle of the Terror* (1932).

Ellery, E., *Brissot* (Cambridge, Mass., 1915).

Gottschalk, L., *Marat* (1927).

———— "Philippe Sagnac and the Causes of the French Revolution," in *The Journal of Modern History,* XX (1948), 137-148.

Greer, D., *The Incidence of the Terror* (Cambridge, Mass., 1935).

Guerlac, H., "Some Aspects of Science during the French Revolution," in *The Scientific Monthly,* vol. 80 (1955), 93-101.

Palmer, R. R., *Twelve Who Ruled* (Princeton, 1941).

Thompson, J. M., *Robespierre*. 2 vols. (1936).

Wendel, H., *Danton* (1935).

Williams, L. P., "Science, Education and the French Revolution," in *Isis,* vol. 44 (1953), 311-330.

THE FRENCH REVOLUTION AND CONTINENTAL EUROPE

Beik, P. H., *The French Revolution Seen from the Right* (Philadelphia, 1956).

Blok, P. J., *History of the People of the Netherlands,* vol. V (1912).

Brinton, C., *A Decade of Revolution, 1789-1799* (1934), chs. 3, 7, and 10.

Gershoy, L., *From Despotism to Revolution, 1763-1789* (1944).

Gooch, G. P., "Europe and the French Revolution," *Cambridge Modern History,* vol. 8 (1904), 754-790.

———— *Germany and the French Revolution* (1920).

Palmer, R. R., "Much in Little: The Dutch Revolution of 1795," in *The Journal of Modern History,* XXVI (1954), 15-35.

———— "The World Revolution of the West, 1763-1801," in *Political Science Quarterly,* LXIX (1954), 1-14. These articles by a leading American historian elaborate the thesis that the French Revolution was part of a larger world movement.

THE UNITED STATES

Faÿ, B., *The Revolutionary Spirit in France and America* (1927).

Hazen, C. D., *Contemporary American Opinion of the French Revolution* (Baltimore, 1897).

Jones, H. M., *America and French Culture, 1750-1848* (Chapel Hill, 1927).

Link, E. P., *Democratic-Republican Societies, 1790-1800* (1942).

Schachner, N., *The Founding Fathers* (1954).

GREAT BRITAIN AND IRELAND

Birley, R., *The English Jacobins from 1789 to 1802* (London, 1924).

Brown, P. A., *The French Revolution in English History* (London, 1918).

Cobban, A., ed., *The Debate on the French Revolution, 1789-1800* (London, 1950).

Hayes, R., *Ireland and Irishmen in the French Revolution* (London, 1932).

INDEX